To Barbara Kindness — Love & Blessings! Dara

Communion with God

Reflections of Life and Love through Spirit

DARA MARIE

BOOK PUBLISHERS NETWORK
Changing the World One Book at a Time

Book Publishers Network
P.O. Box 2256
Bothell • WA • 98041
PH • 425-483-3040
www.bookpublishersnetwork.com

10 9 8 7 6 5 4 3 2 1

Printed in the United States of America

LCCN 2015946832
ISBN   978-1-940598-80-2

Editor: Julie Scandora
Cover designer: Laura Zugzda
Layout: Melissa Vail Coffman

To my beautiful and loving daughter, Kimberly Lorraine.
You give my life higher purpose and meaning.

Pure love never sleeps
It is always awake, thriving, and complete
Go to the ultimate source of all
Drink from the Divine well, absorb
Feel the sweet caress
As love is given and returned
Rejoice in the manifestations

—*Dara Marie*

CONTENTS

PREFACE

The following writings span many subjects that contain messages with special meanings and purpose. They are the reflections of my life, but my experiences also are parallels of all our lives in that everyone encounters challenges and joys, losses and loves that would seem the same but, at the same time, are particularly unique. We can all have appreciation for the same things of our world—for life itself—if we allow it through the expansion of our God-given senses. I have also included at the end of many writings what inspired the work or some additional thoughts.

While some writings will impact your sense of self more than others, many will seem to fit your personal "puzzles" and will bring new light to your own experiences. It can be difficult when we feel forlorn, but we are never truly alone if we have received God and embrace His designs for us.

It was when more quiet times came after my husband passed away that I could let go of self and then allow God energy to fully enter my heart and soul, producing an overwhelming peace. What followed were the results of self-examination, expanded revelations that allowed new insights to surface and made their way to the pages of this work.

I pass on these writings with my heartfelt humbleness that they will comfort, re-enforce, or provide you with whatever it is you may find useful or enlightening.

May the essence from Divine life, truth, and love of our Father continue to manifest upon you, and may these writings remind us all of many things. Seek and ye shall find Him, always. He does not turn away from us, but we sometimes do that to Him. The journey is so much sweeter and easier when we hold onto His hand for . . . everything.

ACKNOWLEDGEMENTS

With a grateful heart, I wish to acknowledge those that have helped me and continue bringing about greater revelations to my presence and for my release through the written word.

I wish to thank in particular Dr. Wayne W. Dyer for his many written works of enlightenment, as well as the Dalai Lama, Joyce Meyers, Esther and Jerry Hicks, Charles Stanley, and Jentezen Franklin. I have obtained greater insight, knowledge, and understanding through their works.

I would be remiss in not including the impact that beautiful music has had on me as well. Music can magnify many things, and it is not my intent to promote only certain artists, but I mention ones whose works impacted me sufficiently in a writing to give them the credit of the inspiration. However, the music of the composer and performer Yanni has definitely put me in a place of higher self, overall, and after listening to his works once more, the writings began.

A special thanks to my daughter Kimberly Lorraine for her faith and ongoing belief that my writings would be published one day. A thank-you as well for my granddaughter, Brenna, for her photograph of me for this work.

Thank you also to Tom Keogh for his unrelenting but constructive remarks after reading some of my writing and for sharing with me the teachings he absorbed from his teacher and mentor, Lady Burttis, after she received her very formal education in London, England, during WWII. Tom has graciously maintained a reasonable amount of patience with me through it all.

I wish also to extend my acknowledgement of and appreciation for my mother, Lucille Elizabeth. She instilled in me at a very young age my spirituality, my appreciation of music, and all the other factors that nurtured my true sense of direction, while allowing me the opportunity for creative expansion in many areas. I feel truly blessed in having had her as my mother.

Almost, but Not to Be

For those that believe in the Divine influence in our lives
We pray to be blessed, also to give and ask to serve our Supreme Father
There are those that then come along in our journey
To touch our lives and their purpose not fully known
The timing and place right but, then again, seemingly wrong

We travel onward with them on the common journey of life
With the sunshine truly felt, flowing down from above
Each heart touched, but the shadows yet to be discovered
When they are embraced and fully uncovered in reality
The human heart cries out as new directions unfold

We then realize through some anguish and even pain
They are not the one meant for us on the continuing path
It is something many of us have to work through
The molding of each one, and He knows the reasons
"Why or why not?" we still humanly ask in heartfelt pain

We ask, why was this person included in our life?
What effect and purpose was there to be for each?
Until we delve deep inside ourselves reaching for the truth
The answers to be found in complete release of mind and heart
In reaching to God alone can they manifest, but we must listen

The mind and heart connect with thoughts and intense emotion
Could this other person finally be our true soul mate?
Are we trying to fit the mold or making the other fit ours?
The process, though painful, does provide for our growth
And the other's growth as well, maybe feeling something unknown

We then have to stop and pay attention to the still quiet voice
Come to terms with our dreams but also face in time reality
We have to trust completely and have absolute faith
And give up someone we may have learned to love and embrace
But the other is not the answer and whom we are really to be with

As time goes on, however brief or long in human time
We all have to open the doors, let the fresh air in, and pause
Relish in the soft breezes gently caressing our being from above
Then once understanding is obtained from what we are to have and gain
We go onward and upward and, in peace and consolation, continue

Then the freedom of the heart and mind embraces more clarity,
      even with regret
Peace and grace once again unfold as a sunrise to heart and soul
The gentle breath of the Divine once more gently felt and needed
As a soft whisper from the mind and heart, "almost, but not to be"
We each then go on, our destiny allowed to be magnified

It is so hard, though, when each destiny is intertwined to some degree
As the journey of life continues onward with human measurement
Love is love, no matter whether this person is truly to be ours
The heart still well remembers the dreams, but not to be
The tears, even from understanding, can still come at any time

      This is a painstaking journey in and of life that many of us will experience. When taken, and the pain subsides, and with continued faith, the fulfillment for our correct person will be presented. Finally, we will understand why "almost, but not to be" should have occurred, in spite of our longings.

ALONE AND EMPTY

One can be and feel so alone at times
In the deep recesses of mind and heart
It matters not whether in a crowd or not
The wrenching feeling of being alone can engulf self

We can all go on feeling lost and empty inside
No matter when someone else tries to help
We all need to fill up our thoughts, our being
And be grateful for what we do have

We need finally to get humanly sick and tired
The overwhelming sense of isolation to be overcome
There was someone that told me long ago
"Pull yourself up by the bootstraps, have no pity party
Dust yourself off mentally, emotionally, and go on"

We are all, at times, presented an unfriendly hand
On this mortal level where we exist now
Reverse the negative thoughts and feelings
Put your feet back firmly on the ground
March onward with confidence, love in your heart

Get over the sense of self-imposed prison from within
Our minds and hearts have so much room
In the simple acts of love and kindness to others
People will be drawn to us, retreat ye not, resume

We also need to go to others and assist when they cry
With support, we need to reach out our loving hand
There are many human beings to be found
With love and kindness; they do come forth

If someone has helped you overcome the loneliness
Spread your wonderful and joyful messages onward
They will do the same for others, rest assured
Before we know it, we are not alone in our mind or heart
And we understand we never really were

And, as the feelings of emptiness depart from us
Actually we are never really singular, as we already know
He is always near and within each of us standing by
Rejoice, behold, and spread your love onward
And, in doing so, the empty feeling is no more in the giving

Love conquers all and radiates outwardly, our choice
The blessings from it in turn continue to heal
Touching our heart and soul in unison as we do others
We are no longer alone, and emptiness is conquered
The trick is in the remembering when it tries to engulf us again

This is something that transpired with me, and still I sometimes do battle with this myself, as feelings of being alone, secluded, especially as I pause to write, create, and prepare for the future manifestations of living and have very little contact with other human beings during the process. But, always trying to maintain love for not only us but also for others and with hope and confidence, we continue on, ever pushing forward. By not allowing the negative energy to grab onto our beings and thwart our God-given right to joys, blessings, we can all come back to our true center core. As He gives to us freely and as we cling to Him, let us all progress and know there is no place within us that is alone and empty. It is up to us as mortals also to do our part mentally, emotionally to know, declare we are indeed not alone or empty, for He fills our hearts and souls with abundant love, which then permits us to extend it onward and be blessed.

DARA MARIE

ALTERING HUMAN DECISIONS

There are many times we are blessed
Moments so sublime and gently presented
Thoughts from Him transmitted to each of us
Through His love they can be quietly received

Answers to our questions or longings
The quiet still voice even reprimanding
That deep inward feeling of knowing
That which is right and wrong in our mind

Each individual senses things differently
Depending upon how tuned in we are
We must all allow the flow from the Creator
The connective wires, if you will, non-corrosive

We each are presented directions
People also enter our lives
It can sometimes be overwhelming
But there are the opportunities
Now the human choice is involved

He gives us all the answers
Or the means by which to overcome
It is our ultimate responsibility, however
And therein lies the true test of us

No matter what the hurdle
For things to conquer or unfold
We each need to do our human part
Our human decisions determine
Steps forward, backward, or just standing still

No one said it would be easy, the human decisions
The challenges of life we all encounter
He gave each human being free will
And now that becomes the toughest part

We must all realize the fresh air
When doors and windows are opened for us
We need then to do and make our human decisions
Or, sadly, as He must often do, patiently wait
The decisions of mortal men and women not doing their part

He, in our having faith, gives us so much
When we go to Him searching and asking
Why then do we each in our stubborn ways refuse
To be uplifted, overcome, and go onward?

The Light is waiting for each one
Demonstrations to be gained and fulfilled
We can miss so much He lovingly presents to us
Our free will over decisions stands in the way

At the crossroads, we often are
At times afraid of our thoughts
By walking the walk of total faith
We can and will overcome all

It is waiting for all mankind, the love
We must recognize at first what has been given
Then with a tender smile of understanding
We say thank you and do our human part

He gives us opportunities all the time, our Creator
Challenges presented or the answers to prayers
But He is ever at our side with love and understanding
We need to go to Him and listen, however, and find strength

Another human decision for us all to make

Anger, Powerful Destroyer

How many times on our mortal journey
That anger has swelled up within us
It takes its toll on the giver and the receiver
But also adds to the dark energy around us

There is a fine line between anger and standing up for right
To someone or something perhaps to get attention
Or is it our own reaction to something or someone?
It doesn't matter, the internal result the same

There is also passion that comes into play
So many things can confuse the senses
I sometimes still need to learn
The many differences there are, oh God, please help me

I do not wish to have anger as such
So hear my prayer asking forgiveness when I do
All I can do is try to learn to differentiate
Between anger and all negative passions stemming from my reactions

I will not, however, make anger my resolution technique
But I will stand up and be counted when necessary
Against all dark energy that would try to claim me or others
My God, my Father, you are my ultimate power

As I Passed You By

Weaving around curves down a beautiful winding road
Out in the free territory leaving intense humanity behind
Relishing in the colors of autumn presented in full array
The road traveled quietly drawing in beauty to the senses

The crisp air, glorious sunshine filtering through the trees
Lining the traveled path like a grand archway of some kind
Leaves fluttered downward, their escape from spring and summer
Now it was time for preparation of renewal once again

I came upon you walking alongside the road, my path
Each one of us having our own destination to seek
You were not much to look at in your present attire
Holding a small bag in one hand on your labored journey

You looked as if you could have used a helping hand
Life had thus far seemed to treat you unfairly perhaps
Or had you been successful at one time in the past?
And now you seemed to have hit rock bottom

Your hair was dirty, clothes as well, and tattered
You certainly had seen better days, I am thinking
Your fall, spiraling downward was quite evident
As you trudged endlessly making your slow headway

I slowly passed you, wondering if I should offer you a ride
In these times, one must be careful, I gently sighed
I glanced over at you, compassion in my eyes
You lifted your weary head and returned a soft smile

What brought you to the place you are now?
I have no idea, of course, because I did not stop
But now I wish I had done it
Given you a ride, some greenbacks, and just listened

DARA MARIE

You might not have accepted my offer of a ride
Perhaps even been reluctant to take money from me
But for some reason, I feel we could have shared much
If only I had stopped and paused on my own journey

I was not in a hurry, and you were not either
I could perhaps have helped you, but somehow I feel
That you could have shared some wonderful things of life
You were soft and gentle, not a threat to me I could tell

How many times have I thought and talked to my inner being
That I wished, after the fact, I had taken just a little more time
To try to help a stranger that crossed my path
But in the end, alas, I did not, and feel badly once again

You got me thinking about my own life
From encountering you alongside the road that day
It reminds me to be so very grateful once again
That I have security, comfort, and been taken care of
My hair, clothes are not dirty or tattered

As the Tide, the Ebb and Flow of Life

I have lived long enough mortally now and pause
To at last understand and to somewhat comprehend
Our positive, negative life occurrences as they flow in and out
As the tide naturally moves, so does our presence

As we exist in this mortal life and form now
We are presented things, situations, others
Reality checks, emotional ups and downs
The tide within us ever moving and constant

The ongoing movement, each having its place
Whether advancing or with our emotional withdrawal
Depending upon how we view, comprehend
Each having its design, the plan of learning, advancing

Each one can fulfill the purpose of ebb and flow
The stimulus in which to grow in understanding
Is the glass half empty, our perception being in question
Or is it half full, we may ponder, feeling what we do

So as our lives progress and in looking deeply into our soul
As we experience our ever-changing tides of emotion, in or out
The movement of each having dominion over us at that time
Emotionally deep inside each one, then expanded recognition

When the tide is out, water has then receded
It offers us much to view, what is otherwise hidden
We can walk the shore and see the treasures of heart, soul
If we do not take the walk, the experience does not happen

When the tide advances, now caressing the shore
More expanse of water seen, the perception different
We can then have that appreciation felt
All is in order, perfect timing and rhythm

When we totally ignore the tides in our lives
The natural ebb and flow of life going to waste
We can miss so much reward, growth, learning of self
Another one of our blessings from the Creator

Conquer the strife and pain in what would manifest
Relish in the sublime, the peace, and the joy
Or as oftentimes happens to all of us
Somewhere it is in-between heaven and earth

Movement of growing for us all, in the seeking

While in quiet reflection living next to the ocean in Anacortes, Washington, and observing the tide gently advance and then retreat, I was presented this writing in soft reflection of the perfect rhythm of life.

Attitude Is a Choice

So many times, we are all confronted with the same challenges in life
The timing of them may vary, but all need to be overcome
We can either allow them credence to harshly impact us
Or step beyond them in going to and with the Divine

Our attitude makes all the difference in attainment
I am discovering this humbly myself, as well, all the time
Whether we allow ourselves just to surrender, our choice
We can give up completely and just state, "Oh well, my lot in life"
Or try, with our Source, to conquer what needs to be done

We need to place ourselves in complete faith, ah, the test
Above and beyond, tackling our human thoughts and inclinations
Even though we may be emotionally crushed, our limit reached
Hold firm in declaration and gain greater understanding
The why, the how we have allowed something to disrupt

Our attitudes so important toward the final result attainable
Perhaps we have been willful in allowing things to alter
Something or someone impacting our lives, not a good choice
We have all encountered; I myself still struggle with some
And will, I am sure, on the journey, have more to deal with

We must all look deeply and honestly within ourselves
It is not an easy process for us to accomplish
In order to find out, at times, how we have permitted
Something or someone to throw us in turmoil, pain
But, no matter the challenge, we must continue on with progress

Cling to God, our Source, first and foremost, I also remind myself
We must make our connection true and strong as best we can
It is a continuing process all of the time, always the challenge
In doing this and at least trying to forge ahead with faith
Many times, we are protected from encountering them at all

Every situation that deprives, hurts, or binds us in any way
Can be handled and turned around with diligence from us
Our attitude so important, though, as I have to also keep in mind
Are we willing to do our human work for greater attainment?

Our ultimate Source, our strength, our guide
Is patiently waiting for us all to make our connections
It is a continual process, and each day important
To make sure the connection is not corroded from whatever may happen
We are all indeed the same and, oh, how human in our struggles

Awaken, Love Is All

God cries out to His people
You say you love Me
But mankind, you find it so hard
To treat your fellow man as I have asked
Love has sometimes been abandoned

In love, I have given to you
The world in which you live
Its beauty for you all to behold
In magnificence and splendor
Each region unique, its own

In appreciation, you must remain
Abandon Me not
Remember Me in all that you are
In all that you do
I am always near
Lean upon Me and awaken

Love for each other continually given
My children, you all are
Look upon one another
As an expression and reflection of Me
Oh, My children, awaken

Each earthly region you now dwell in I have given you
And the people of these lands must be able to live and determine
In their own way, in their own creed
United in peace and united with harmony
Not seeking to overrun others
But seeking and progressing in and with their own abilities

Dara Marie

Each nationality left to your own
To honor Me, the Divine Creator
In your own way
Each of you being fulfilled
Oh, please awaken, for all

In peacefulness and reverence for one another
My will to be accomplished
Each child of Mine unique
Reflections of truth and love divine
Care for My Earth, your home
Care for each other
Oh, please, awaken more love

The Awakening

A life so immersed
So directed by one
Emotions of joy
Emotions of pain

Feeling of helplessness
Watching, waiting
Anticipation, not knowing
When will the end come?
Mortal existence no more

The moment coming unexpectedly
The time called home
Peacefulness at last
Release of human form

Fly with the angels
Be with God
Oh, glorious release
No more hurting
No more pain
Whole at last, complete again

In peaceful reflection
The next level taken
Further understanding
Revelations, a new attainment

Renewal of soul
Glad tidings for you
Release of me
Awakening for both
Each level unfolding

Barefoot with Thorns

Seemingly an angelic being here on earthly plane
You have done great deeds at one time, or so it would seem
Then the mortal dark energy you allowed in yourself
Once an angel, barefoot, and of pure intent
Now sadly, as a very enlightened Native American has stated
Thorns are upon your feet and allowed to take over

There are many, it would seem, around, but you, my first encounter
In the guise of pronouncing they are truly Divinely led, and obedient
How many have decided to allow dark energy inside their core?
Beguiled by other than pure love and truth, the Divine elements
Even though you stated that is where you come from and are
Your actions no longer warrant the declarations you made

You came into my mortal life in order simply to use and take
To gain what you could from me with and in pure selfishness
You were always the center of the talk and actions present
Self-propelling, you now have become, as you have accused others
Oh, the illusion of being an angel here on earth in doing good works
Now the thorns you have, by your actions, shown

Those that try to follow the true path with diligent resolve
In purer thoughts, words, and yes actual deeds done
In giving of one's heart, soul to and for others, love
We cling tightly, and on guard ourselves, we must be
That no thorns extend from our own feet with time
So that we remain in and with our proper alignment with God

Those that are succeeding stay close to the Creator
Constantly on a united front, we must all maintain help for each other
Not let our own self enter too much within our beings
Continually go on in the Divine way of all things
In order not to permit thorns, attachments to our own feet
Truly to bless others with unselfish acts and deeds

To let go of self in all that we do and are, we at least try
To be true caregivers to all we encounter with love
And to be continually, as well, on Divine and mortal guard
For others appearing barefoot, but thorns exposed at last
In which to use, take, try to manipulate, and then flee
When we might push back or revolt, manageable by you no more

It sometimes takes mortal time to have the thorns exposed
For others finally to get what you are all about, the reality
But, in keeping our proper alignment with the Creator
With pure intent, love, and truth being clung to above all else
We are protected, guided, and directed in what to do
The warning signs are given to us from above, as were mine

Yes, there were warning signs from the beginning from you
You clearly dangled many things in front of me with enticement
Thinking I might take the bait in full measure
You did not, however, realize my sense of true direction
I allow my Father, you see, to be ever at my side
And, I listen to the Supreme Voice over all others

Oh pretending angel, now in disguise, barefoot you are no more
You yourself exposed the thorns you now have unfortunately
You almost led me astray, but I am so grateful for not following
The lesson you taught me from your own thorns upon your feet
I now take with me, and in gratefulness, I say thank you
Not to you necessarily but my Father, Creator of us all, for protection

I could have whined and complained, feeling sorry for what I gave
But, I take this lesson to heart, you see, and needed it apparently
I still cling to the Ultimate Light above all else daily
With pure intent in my own heart and soul, I only desire
His light allows no thorns to grow when we are sincere
And, here again, I thank you for the mortal lesson shown

I must continue on the right path with persistence and faith
And be ever watchful and on guard all of the time
To continue with and in the Light Supreme with love
Reflection of the Divine presence, the Divine energy
Of the Creator Supreme, Father of us all, I pray and declare
I will not allow or permit thorns to extend from me

I will every mortal day continually cling to Him
And try my very best to reflect the pure light given to all
I also pray for you as well with love, of course, as He represents
That your thorns will somehow disappear one day
And you can be brought back and with pure reflection
To do God's work and, yes, be blessed for your unselfish efforts

But, if not, that is your determination and your mortal choice
I have enough to do in being watchful myself, thank you
So that thorns do not try to grasp at me, turn me around
I pray that others who are with the same presence
Will be protected and guided with our Father's abiding love

"Barefoot with thorns" is a Native American Lakota expression, which was stated to me when I relayed the above circumstances of this work to a spiritual leader in North Dakota. The term, as explained to me, refers to someone who pretends to be something he or she truly is not, even with the guise of possessing Divine-realm attributes and insights. One must guard against this kind of human being, and as I have stated through this work, I was protected from further harm but always remain on guard for the next time I encounter someone barefoot with thorns.

Beautiful Arched Garden Gate to the Meadow

From the new beautiful land obtained
I look down the path from the main house
Toward the arched gate below
The sunshine now upon it . . . meadow beyond
Oh so beautiful and grand you are

It is a special place from the native presence of long ago
Peaceful, serene, and having a spiritual essence
Visitors are automatically drawn to it
As if seeking a threshold to something beyond
To pause and rest the weary soul

When I first came upon you
And walked under your lovely archway
Unlocking the gate, I walked into the meadow
I felt the sense of relinquishing all cares and worries
It is like embracing the oneness with God

It is really hard to totally describe the experience
The feeling that one so easily and deeply absorbs
But there must be something to it
Because I am not the only one
It beckons one to it, this arched, wooden garden gate

The path to it curves through forest green
The tranquility from this alone is felt
A magic sense of no mortal time, the ancient ones present
A most special place just to rest
The weary heart and soul of one

One can almost equate the peace
To the quiet abandonment of Heaven
Once the gate is opened and you step through the portal
You feel God's presence all around
A most magical place indeed, the little meadow beyond

So come and visit if you will
And you too will be captivated
Be drawn toward this special spot
Other human beings meeting a bit of heaven
This feeling experienced by all drawn to it

I am so grateful for this tranquil spot
Even though harsh weather elements may dim my view
The pure essence is still present
As one looks down the winding path from my home
To the arched gateway to peace and tranquility present

The author of this creative work
So hopes each reader can find
Your own symbol of restful freedom
And, in doing so, become closer to God
And let Him touch you oh-so gently and sweetly

Beautiful Roaring, Cascading Water of Life

The human beings approach my beauty and my thunderous noise and spray
Positioning themselves down on the surrounding rock in awe of my grandeur
I am beautiful, but I wonder if many will see beyond me and look onward
In thought and retrospection at many things besides the water of life

I am made up of so many water droplets as they gather to form me
Each one making and encompassing the whole and bringing forth my beauty
When they all come together in presenting the wonderful thing you see
The effect, the whole, is quite striking, don't you think?

Each droplet then becomes so much more for the whole result, me
As I am just one grand performance of many here on Earth
The roar and movement delights and brings so much to the senses
Oh, but there is so much more to behold and become for others

You can think of each droplet as a human being here on Earth
In mass and together making up something that I am now
Strength, joy, and the peaceful tranquility of being beautiful
Even the rocks that surround me have been smoothed down with power

Such a grand spectacular thing I have become, and I can grow
The senses are awakened from sight and sound, and how wonderful
I am just one event here on our mortal plane, which I contribute to
You have to realize that even without being here yourself, I am grand

More droplets are always being added, which give me further magnitude
They continue rushing onward and cascading down to their destination
I may be hidden from view from so many human beings now, and in the past
They do not know where I am, but now I have been blessed by you

I am very proud of being created and continually fed by my droplets
Each one important for the result of the whole, the total accomplishment
I wish more human beings could do the same while they are here
How grand their sight and sounds could become in the scheme of things

I will continue as long as I am fed and nourished from my source
The roaring droplets you see are the key to make me flourish, become grander
When and if the water-of-life droplets cease to feed and nourish me
I will just become a small trickle and of minimal beauty and consequence
You may perhaps not even see me again for nourishment, beauty, and joy

Bending in Life as a Reed in the Wind

A life transpires through our journey
Human will pushes against us
We do not always understand
Why things sometimes fail to materialize

We so often ask, "Why not?"
From God/Creator, Who we believe is in control
But then a door will open for us
And we say, "This is so much better than I thought"
More than we wanted or hoped for

Like a reed swaying in the wind of life
We must learn to gently bend
Human will pushed aside
And allow ourselves to be divinely led

If we are too firm and rigid
The reed will not then bend
If our human will is so powerful
We may even snap at times
With the harsher winds of life we encounter

Let us all pray to our Heavenly Father
From where our guidance comes
Release and feel His love
The love ever-present from the great I Am

Let us all be still and listen
And go to the place where we may hear
And know that He will guide and direct
Our every true need being fulfilled
The right direction is perfectly presented

The Blending of Two from a Dream

As I look into your eyes
So gentle are they
I see beyond to your inner soul
All that you are
All that I am
The tenderness intertwined
From God's eternal power

I see beyond; the mist no more
The human will of self is compromised
The gifts we each have to give and pass on for others
Unrelenting is their quest for surrender
Each one of us to a higher purpose of service
In his or her own way
United in love
Oh, how blessed

Each heart hurts
The other not knowing
How can we then be brought together?
For love's unfurling

Upon a hill I am standing
Overlooking the sea
Marveling at its beauty
That God has indeed given

You see me from afar, eyes meeting
Each heart throbbing
Both in wonderment upon the other
Gently smiling
Love's grand encounter

"Oh, what will I say?"
Each soul confiding
So that I may in gentleness be sharing
My heart, my life, my being
Each one cries out inwardly

What do I do?
Not to show how I feel
Not let on how I am
The reflection of you
The blending of two
Instantly recognized
One to another
My heart be still, if only for a moment

Then we come to one another
Soft smiles each
Hands touching gently
Then a kiss
Oh, my soul mate
Welcome to my world
I want no other

The longing, the waiting no more
Each heart tightly intertwined
The perfect blend
Each one bringing his or her full measure
The glasses of desire now full
The peace overwhelming

Bob and Weave, I Am a Playful Sea Otter

I am such a lovable creature, and you know it
Yes, I absolutely know I am, I say with glee
I'm a rascal; that is for sure, oh well
I do all sorts of cute and goofy antics

I am in certain seas, as well as rivers
Put me in water, and I am just fine, thank you
But, I also like to be on land just a little
To see what trouble I can get into, oh my

When I have snow to play in, oh, the delight
The game of slip and slide is on, that is for certain
I romp up to the top of perhaps a hill
Oh goody, I get to slide all the way down

While in the sea, I love kelp beds, you know
I dive and find perhaps a tasty morsel just for me
Then I need to keep track of my darn rock
On my back I go, float, and pound my morsel upon it

Then after that task is done, off I go once again
Either to play, find more food, or just whatever
I bob and weave in playfulness with others
I'm also very cute, I must say, while doing it

So many years ago, men hunted me so
For my fur, and they did delight in it
Other creatures were also set upon
Some actually almost were entirely gone

I am protected now from mankind, except for pollution
There are many types set upon me, you know
I hope they are more careful, but I wonder
Each day, depending upon my location, can be dangerous

Until something happens, though, I just bob and weave
I will remain carefree and playful through it all
I just cannot help the way I am, you know
That is how and what the Creator made me to be

I'm just a little goofy, I am thinking, oh well
I do not care much if others think I am
I have my own agenda and things to do
I'm always busy, frisky, I am

Now where is my darn rock again? Hmmmm

Living by the sea and being allowed to watch these lovable creatures, I found this writing coming to me one afternoon while viewing them playfully surrendering themselves among a vast bed of kelp. It also brings to mind the plight of so many species that live at the mercy of human beings, and we must try to protect them from harm.

BOMBARDMENT

From the outside world you come
Whether from media, people, or circumstances
Apprehension, false fear of the unknown
Oh, disruptive one—negative energy the culprit

At what point do we reclaim the peacefulness within us?
It is so needed in this time of our worldly upheavals and strife
The power that calms the screaming voice within
We come back and declare our spiritual connection

Many times, all I say quietly to myself, as my mother taught me
Within my special mental realm of seeking more peace
"God directs; His love protects," a most powerful statement
Then in and with full belief, I go on

There are some days when much is needed
In trying to be alert against the negative thief
I simply say these few words in declaration
But, oh, the powerful statement made

At times the immediate results not seen
To the mortal presence or perception
In Your time, not mine, Supreme Father
I place myself, my trust in You for my manifestations

How many times I have waited repeating the statement
Most anxiously in anticipation for the results
Even fighting against some mortal fear within
You, the great I Am, I know will purge the dark clouds for me

From Your radiant sunshine, the true direction
That one of Your children should take
The paths, the doors are opened
And the correct answers, fulfillment always given

I wait on You still with even more faith and resolution
Whether a small or large mountain to be climbed
With even one small positive declaration being stated
I reaffirm my alignment with the Divine, my Creator

So each day, I will claim victory
I put You in control of all things
The turbulence, bombardments cease; then quiet attainment
From and with Your love, direct and protect me I pray

The Book of Life, Truth, and Love

I am a book, my cover quite something really and holding many things
Each one of my pages has a gold-tipped edge carefully placed on it
The pages beautiful with insights, lessons, demonstrations, healing
They lovingly are presented to each man and woman here on Earth

I am a book of existence, beautiful in concept and holding truth
My cover is very strong in presence but also can be very soft and pliable
Each page, as it unfolds, a possible step to growth toward the ultimate
Each human being with the desire to be nurtured should read all of
      my chapters

Until you arrive at the end of the book, and hopefully enlightenment attained
Each one holding lessons, understanding, and answers to questions
Each page and chapter unfolding something separately, but also for the whole
You, as a mortal human being, also have to take and allow the direction given

Each chapter holds a key for learning, advancement, healing, and
      demonstration
What you go through in your own life sometimes drastically affects others
You also have to be able to grasp and draw from the pages, the messages
The lessons are sometimes harsh, depending upon your individual need

One of the harshest lessons in my book of life is one all have to endure
A dream you might have for yourself, and then reality is at last embraced
The heart and emotions coming to terms; as a dream fades away
You then scream from within, "Why, oh why is it not working out?"

There is much hurt, the very core of you then feeling threatened
You were so hopeful that this was indeed the answer for you
For your longing, your life, it would so alter and become better
Only to realize oh so much strife and eventually not a good thing

You do not totally understand as the pain swells within you and tears come
So many more questions now than answers are coming to the surface
"Oh, dear Lord," you cry out, "but I want it so and please give to me
Why was this door opened to me in the first place? I do not understand"

You try and try to come to human terms with it all; confused you still seek
You plead and cry to Heaven, "If it could only just be, I would be happy"
You must all realize that no matter how hard it is humanly to grasp
You must step back and just have the faith there is a better, higher purpose

Even though you may wrench from the events and effects of not obtaining
You all must have the faith and believe this is not the best result for you
A lesson in a chapter of my book closes, as if a door is slammed in your face
Another better answer or circumstance does in fact wait in the future

In time, you will be able to heal, more fully understand and comprehend
Each one of you has a different time line in which to grow and advance
My chapters are here not to punish you but to provide for your growth
There is a reason, a lesson to be learned and contained from each one

It is up to each individual soul, however, to have the faith to let go
To turn and advance to each new chapter, fully embracing its contents
What each one holds and demonstrates is another lesson to be learned
Sometimes, however, until we learn, the same chapter is repeated over
        and over

The writer of this creative work is not here to preach, as it also applies to me
I have my own chapters to learn from and then go on toward the
        waiting lessons
We are presented a book, and we all have to encounter our own chapters
Life, truth, and love wait for us all with beautiful gold-tipped pages

Broken Vows

How I loved you so, or was it an illusion?
I myself gave you more credit and attributes of character than you had
When we were joined, we both took sacred vows
Declaring our love, united for mortal time

Then the years and life started slipping away
A child, and then you started to stray
I still do not understand why it happened
But soon, the struggle of unity took over

Many years of trying to make things work
Leaving the sanity of mind, heart, and soul
You always promised to be good once again
But, in the end, there were too many vows broken

To this day, I do not understand you at all
Perhaps you do not fully even know yourself
There seems to be so much of this going on
Is it the human beings involved, times we live in?

I cried and was in torment for so many years
I know I could have perhaps tried harder myself in some things
We were both so young when Cupid's arrows struck hearts
But when the young passion calls, we leap too fast

So many hours of talking about plans for the future
I still look back now and dimly remember our wedding day
Dreams now long since dashed upon the rocks
Sacred vows taken at the time, long since have drifted away

We are now different, or were we even then?
We just did not realize it, too much passion in place of love
Now many years have devoured our lives
Just as sacred vows, feelings for you a dim memory

Bubble Wrap

As I was packing one day for a move
This thought came to me as I quietly worked
Bubble wrap surrounds and protects many things
Such a simple idea to embrace, divinely speaking

Before getting into the car for a journey
Or confronting a potential weather situation
Whatever arises giving us apprehension or being afraid
Declare our bubble-wrap Divine protection in place

Then my thoughts wandered even more
We can choose what color of duct tape we wish
To keep the wrap securely in place around us
Mine is actually all the colors of the rainbow

Kind of a catchy symbolic thought declaration
But just getting in the habit of saying these two words
We put out the positive declaration for His protection
And then, with faith, we let God do the rest

Whatever situation or circumstance you may find yourself experiencing
Declare you are protected and aligned with Him
Bubble wrap is easy to remember
And then you tape it around you with imaginary duct tape

And then you can change your duct tape color anytime you wish!

DARA MARIE

THE BUTTERFLY

The butterfly flutters here and there
Searching for this and that
Stopping every once in awhile
To rest its weary wings

Butterflies are so beautiful
Each one being unique
Different sizes and colorings
All demonstrating the same dance

They are so delicate and fragile
I am captivated by their individual beauty
Watching them doing their graceful ballet in the air
Each one on its own but much the same mission

How like a butterfly we are
Each soul unique, with our individual beauty
All of us searching for this and that
But all having to rest our own weary wings

Their existence here on Earth so brief
We are amazed why that is so
But when we stop and think about it
So are we in the scope of things

The Capability of Feeling Love at All

My heart and soul have cried out so many times
Why have I been so touched, so hurt?
I have lost loves in the past
They have come and now are gone

So many expectations, oh, the feelings of joy
Being with another, being so deeply touched
I have hurt so before; I have mourned the losses
Now I wonder, do I want to go through that again?

I have to remember each time it happened
How I felt deeply within me, my heart and soul
Promises made by others were never kept
I felt so deeply betrayed, once again

Then others were presented in my life
Should I, could I once again even want to love?
Some choices were made stemming from my needs
Looking back, they should not have even been

My last love, even though humanly the journey so hard
So many things to try to overcome .
The love that was there in the beginning
Towards the end was different from that at first

He has now moved onward
To a different level of existence, his expansion
I do miss the love, the closeness once felt
The sharing, the caring, the gentle touches

In looking back on the ones in my life
Who have been, who have come and gone
In feeling the loss, I at last understand
I had enough love in me and do now
To feel the losses at all; some do not

This poem was inspired by "Learning from Loss" by musician David Templeton in his CD *The Crossing*.

THE CODE OF LIVING

There are many who say one thing and do another
Even quote from their spiritual source and sayings
Passed on lovingly to and for future generations from others
To have and to hold and base a code upon mortal living

We tell others what we feel they must do and be
How they should act, and criticize them at times
But how can we truly reflect the Divine, our Creator
If we do not ourselves live by the "Code of Living"?

There are so many stories and declarations to mankind
Explanations of living that we should all project
We all need to remember, however, within our being
It is easier said than done on our mortal journey
That is the real test for each of us while here on Earth

Cast not the first stone, it has been declared by Him
If we are without sin ourselves, then we can truly do that
I know only one who is so pure, full of unending love
Look to the heavens, to the truth, the Creator of man

Live the Code of being and doing in your daily lives
It must be for all, not just a chosen few here on earthly plane
But it is for everyone to adhere to, no matter where we reside
To hold dear to our hearts and demonstrate to all others

When our mortal existence is no more and we go beyond
We all go onward, we believe, to the Higher Source
We then ourselves are found guilty or absolved of sinful ways
Our human lives are presented before each one of us

Let us then live the Code to all we may encounter along the way
The best we possibly can and become more one with the Divine elements
One with Him, His love radiating outwardly from us
Lest we be harshly judged and the Divine determinations be made

DARA MARIE

COLD WHITE LACE

There is nothing like
A soft snowfall to delight
Lace, each one unique
Falling gently from above

To be in a place
Stillness galore
Quietly standing and watching
The sense of peace within
Behold the sense of God

As the lace accumulates
Building on the ground
The wonder from taking it all in
You do not want to disturb
The beautiful layers of lace

You stand transfixed
They continue to silently fall
The peacefulness, contentment
The gentleness felt deep within
As the lace continues the journey down

It is time to finally depart
You are cold, but warmth felt inside
Watching the white lace fall
Hesitation, then one last look
Departure, but not from God within

The colors of autumn are now showing
Leaves in colorful abandonment
Gently floating and falling
Crisp cold nights
Sunshine during the day
Life's cycle unfolding
What beauty in God's way

As they fall to the ground
Gently floating, drifting down
Life for them on earth
The cycle completed
To replenish and nurture
The next step—onward

During a brief interlude
New buds forming
Ready to grow, they unfold
Life possessed and expressed anew

In looking at the new growth
We pause and reflect
That is the way with us
Cycles completed
Then rebirth—nourishment
To go on and bless with renewal

Colors on the Canvas

A blank canvas stands alone
Then the artist approaches
Paint waiting to be applied
A creator's thought and imagination
Then applied by the steady, gentle hand

As each color is applied one at a time
The canvas becomes bare no more
Colors exploding, as they take shape and form
Making the canvas come alive

Little by little, the artist brings to life
What the imagination wants to portray
The canvas becomes radiant and full of colors
Beautiful images from them demonstrated

I think of us as a blank canvas
Then as our Creator applies all of His colors to us
If we absorb, radiate, and magnify Him
We can become beautiful and vibrant
Another priceless piece of art has been accomplished

This was inspired for my beautiful daughter, Kimberly, and one of her children, Brenna, as they themselves create. They have also become, with their allowance, a most beautiful canvas upon which God is displaying His vast colors.

Complete Delight in the Midst of a Raging Storm

The winds howled, the waves cresting, white lather seen
In amazement, I stood watching this in quiet abandonment
The natural forces taking control of the sea in front of me
The astounding and explosive performance was fascinating

To my amazement while watching this take place
A little flock of small birds descended upon the swirling sea
Calmly placing their tiny forms upon what was so turbulent
I thought, are they putting themselves in harm's way?

These six little birds calmly set themselves down in earnest
Into the turmoil, white crested foam, as the wind continued to howl
No fear expressed and absolutely no concern on their part
They calmly were enjoying the up-and-down ride with glee

They would disappear, engulfed by the turbulent, thrashing sea
Where did they go, I asked myself repeatedly, straining my eyes
And then upon the crest of the next wave in perfect unison
They returned once more into my view, and I just gently smiled

I watched them for quite some time, it seemed
I was transfixed as they calmly were having their fun
I thought to myself, why cannot human beings do the same
Be so at peace, no fear expressed in complete assurance

How easy it is for us to be so fearful and apprehensive
As the angry sea and waves try to thrash us in life
We should and can be more like these little birds
In trusting our Source, we could ride the angry waves

Why do we persist in thrashing about so many times?
These little birds were not fearful, and in pure delight
They trusted they were and would be protected
Oh, human beings, if we could only completely believe as well

Complete Surrender: The Prayer to God and the Hope for Mankind

In the quiet stillness of a dark room early one morning
I came to God on my knees
I prayed to my Creator, omnipotent supreme

I gave Him tribute for my well-being
Gratitude abundant
Softly spoken words of understanding
His footsteps in the sand

My heartfelt tears
My heartfelt pain
Asking his forgiveness
For my so-human ways

I asked Him that night to grant me one request
That I might serve Him and reflect
His love, truth, and tenderness
In all things while still here on earth

I gave Him my pledge
To quietly listen to his calming voice
Nourishing my heart and soul
I asked to be useful, in whatever way
To not leave this world without
Somehow making it a better place

And then my thoughts were redirected
To encompass mankind, oh mankind
You are forgetting His ways
Love for one another
Peace and grace

You take from Mother Earth with little regard
You trample on her beauty
Consuming, destroying, not giving
Mankind, oh mankind
How selfish you are

The battle is on, the war to be won
Mankind must be reminded of God's true love
Evil is gaining; like sheep we are
Following blindly the messages of darkness

His light shines brightly, but we all must embrace
His tenderness, love, and grace
For all to witness, mankind with love
The world united, the world in peace
How wonderful a place it would be

He would then look down on His creations
And at last say
"How grand indeed are my reflections"
I pray, I surrender and will keep the faith
That it can be done; it is the hope I maintain

CONTENTMENT

So many things in a past life
Fear of the unknown, hesitation
At last, I am free now
I do not feel alone

To contemplate where I was
Such a seemingly short time ago
Embracing life now as never before
The path, my passion, unfolding

I am so anxious to be on my new way
Freedom from fear and hesitation
Things now being presented as never before
It is not hard because in faith I am

Feelings have surfaced now in me
Hidden away so long, I think
Or perhaps I never had them before
Now I taste my freedom from bondage

Like an eagle, floating on the waves of air
Gliding, swooping, soaring in pure delight
Ever mindful of time gone by
But content with whom I am becoming now

Since writing this, many things have happened as life continues onward, and even during a pause of motion, one can always gain growth with a positive attitude, and much reflection from and with that allowance. As the Greek saying goes, "As I grow older, I am still being taught."

Cotton-Candy Clouds

Entering a manmade machine, up I climb
Pushing against the earth forces of gravity
Onward we go to rise above the clouds
Then looking down, a feeling of peace, tranquility

Whether in an airplane, glider, hot-air balloon
The ecstasy and sense of departure from the cares of the world
We realize how small we humans really are
The limitless space, peace really astounding

Even when seemingly restrained by a small window
We can see so much endless beauty all around
It is truly amazing, we say, as we mentally drift away
Endless horizon and then reality, outer space

The colors incredible, so many different shades
Then glancing down at the clouds as we go by
We can picture the angels romping and playing
Swooping this way and that, as the imagination takes over

So many shapes, curves, twists, and turns
A ballet of cotton, wispy, playful at times
We want to be able to stretch our hand down to them
To play with the special fluffy cotton candy below

In a glider or hot-air balloon, up, up away
More acute sensations of freedom and silence
An entirely different perspective can be had
As the fluffy cotton candy appears and passes by

The effect, through whatever the human machine
Emotions and senses are heightened beyond mortal
We feel God's presence, and the angels are gleeful
Playing and darting in the cotton-candy clouds

Dara Marie

Dare to Believe and Dream

When we are humanly tired and weary from trying
The spirit and mind tend to digress and just withdraw
It is time to pause and reflect inside, dig deeply within
Do not make the human mistake of pushing onward

The skies may seem dark, and the thunderclouds intensify
All direction seems lost, oh the weary heart and soul
Rest yourself and find the true comfort given to all
Never mind what others may try to do or say

Stand down and renew; God is always present at our side
Even though we may humanly seem to be confused
So many questions; where are the answers?
We must never forget that another also questioned

Take this cup from me, even though my pledge made
The pledge to Thee, I did make, through my heart and soul
I must remain true to the missions I have before me
My destiny is indeed in the hands of the Almighty

I did not strike a bargain with Him but asked to serve
To be used to make this world a better place before leaving
I must now release all doubts and false apprehensions
For my Father in Heaven already knows the answers

He has guided and cared for me all the past moments
Sometimes I doubt myself, reluctant to continue on
Determination, resolve, and now my passion renewed
I dare to believe that He will guide and surround me

When I was with another soft, gentle heart and being
Not long ago, his words touched my heart and soul
"Find your dreams, believe they are true, and find you"
We have all come so far and can receive and know what to do

He would not put us in harm's way but will protect
In fulfilling what He told me to do when having peaceful commune
The human being now must totally release again
I now once again know, believe, and pick up speed

I feel Him smiling down on me as He does to others
Through another dear and gentle soul who has helped me
The heart and mind now once again are at peace
I dare to believe the dreams will certainly be achieved

The voice spoken so gently from his presence
Almost a whisper in saying, "Find your dreams"
I believe, once again, and now am humanly rested
Oh why, oh why did I allow myself doubt?

I stepped back and allowed myself time to pause
Now I am ready to go on in what I must do
The mind, rested once again in peace and resolve
I hope others can and will do the same when needed

Dark Intruder Presence

Oh dark intruding presence, you still persist
Being allowed to continue on by others in what they do
With the persistent shroud you silently come in disguise
Once again in pretense of having credible presence

You pretend, as if to say, it is not you, no, it must be another presence
But know full well you have been unmasked for some time
Many people have already been disarming you
Yes, we must all stand firmly in the truthful realm

You see, we pray for all that have been taken over, oh dark intruder
Yes, we divinely elevate them all just the same and, in so doing, disarm
The task now for each one of us, banded together in unity of purpose
Is not to permit, from our own allowance, any withdrawal

I, for one, stand up to you, maintaining love in my heart
That alone states who and what I am, as others do
I will personally turn the other cheek if I must
But I also will not permit you to upset me any further

In giving you a sense of power by allowing you even to upset me now
Perhaps your perception and certainly not the truth
In even typing this, I am flatly stating to myself and others
I will not even allow you to touch me emotionally, one way or the other

Thus, when we do this, your seeming power is destroyed
You still try to keep pushing in, though, with your dark intruding ways
Now another playground, me, you think you have again
But I will tell you one thing, evil dark intrusion
I no longer give you any power over me, whatsoever

I still am praying for all to be freed of you
And, in doing so, I remain with the Light
Even when you try to destroy it with your deceitful ways
You cannot because you have no further power
Because I and others give you none, and that is power

The Dawning of a New Beginning

I used to think, as a human mother
I needed to stay, continue to watch and protect
My beautiful daughter and her children
To not allow my own expansion of life

I need to go on with my own direction
Now that a freedom has been presented to me
To go out into the world and not stagnate
Reflect God, of course, but also rediscover my own identity

For so many years I fussed, I tried to watch over
My daughter, my beautiful flower from God
I tried to nurture and protect, and I still do what I can
But the mother has learned; the child can as well

What I have said to her occasionally returns to me
Out of her own words, she reminds me when needed
I gently laugh when she says my own words back
Then adds, "As you have told me, Mother"
Funny how that works at times

Roles reversed once more in and with love
I, indeed, take it all in, as I pause
Reflecting in and with appreciation
What my beautiful daughter has said
My own words for her, once again, stated

I will start my new life, a new freedom at hand
My feet now set on a new path, opportunities
To reflect Him and listen, as I cling to my Father
To the calming voice, as I start a new beginning

I yearn to be wanted and needed, as others do
By someone, oh-so sweet and gentle
But also to do His work in what I can accomplish
To be of use to mankind on our blue marble

Not in my ego but in love I go
To serve and receive much joy
Enabling me, a daughter of Him
To gently spread love around to all
And in the giving, it is returned back to me

As we all can search, reach toward the Divine realm
We can allow a new dawning, a new beginning
It is never too late for any of us to continue on
To be blessed, give blessings to others, as a new life emerges
A new dawn upon the heart and soul

Awakening and allowing for a new beginning

This writing emerged after my husband, John, continued on his journey from mortality to his Father. I found myself alone, wondering where my life was going then, or should go. Three months after he departed and having the mindset in place that I would just be on call for my small family, something inside me just could not accept or allow it to continue, as I released one night in complete abandonment to Him, my Father. I hope this writing will bless others that might have that same mindset and allow for their own new beginning of life, as God surely wants us to continue, grow, be blessed, and find renewal once again.

The Deepest Water

When something in life jolts our heart, soul, and existence
Whether the reality an outcome of our own doing or not
Or, perhaps, because of what someone else did or did not do
We need to find the strength and courage within us
To be totally honest with ourselves in pursuit of answers

It is not easy, taking this task on, when we hurt and ache
Finding the courage to dig deeply within our inner core
To come to terms with the seemingly unfavorable outcome
Perhaps it is something within us that added to the result

We all must be truthful, content in figuring out what happened
Wanting to really pursue the correct and truthful answers
We are not perfect human beings, any of us, as we walk the walk
But we can try to do so much better as we journey on

The Source, from above, where we draw the pure water of life
So very deep, there is such an unending supply for all on Earth
In coming to terms with our circumstances and understanding
We need to keep lowering our buckets into the well of truth
And drawing the deeper water out from Him, love for us

There are many currents that run deeply within each core
As the ebb/flow of the material Earth's tides come and go
Eventually, it is all for one ultimate purpose and planned
The constant movement so that the water does not stagnate

So it is with human beings, the deepest waters within us all
We must try to keep the water as clear as we possibly can
With that, we allow our Creator to do this purification for us
But we also must constantly lower our hearts and souls into the well

It takes work, all of the time, as our lives, like the tides, ebb and flow
The constant movement, swirling in-between the still waters
The natural occurrence helps us keep our thoughts ever moving
Evermore trying to find the true answers, truth, and revelations

When we finally come to terms with honesty and directness
Putting aside hurt, and yes, sometimes our own pride
In pursuing clarity, we can finally reach the calmer water
After going deeply inside ourselves, into the deepest water
Then the answers found, clarity, purification, and peace

 This poem was inspired by *The Deepest Water* CD by musician and composer David Templeton.

THE DENSE MIST OVERCOME

I often reflect about my testy moods
They seem to come and go at will
Frantically trying to control me
My every thought, my every move

I must recognize these moods of mine
Push them aside and know
I am to be God's reflection
In thoughts and deeds expressed
Evil to control no more

I must work at it when the dense mist intrudes
To be on guard, reverse, to feel His love
To be able to fully radiate
The good things given to me
I know are from above

Oh, our Heavenly Father, God
I go to you with love
Please let me gratefully receive
In full measure from you
Your tender, gentle, and true love

When I do this and make the effort
Heaven's reflection radiates indeed
Through me to all, I hope
A gentle word, a gentle touch
I then feel so complete and in peace

From time to time a test of wills
Is mine human or from the Divine?
I must give up my human willfulness
In order to, yes, express the Divine

To be in control of myself once more
To give all things up to you
The guidance received with thankfulness
Expressed by my creator, God, to me

I then sense such peacefulness
Oh, the wonderful love received
To be able to give it to others
Through words, thoughts, and deeds

I so long for the world to know
To be able to recognize such love
Whatever you are humanly called
The same true essence received by all

It seems to have become a new age
The longing and grasping by so many
Human beings looking for answers
Now again being discovered—revelations

The test for so many of us
While here in our mortal form
The true revelations expressed through love
Now need to be reacted upon

We need to overcome so many things
Our watchfulness every moment a must
To indeed be able for us to express
The beautiful love from You given to all

For love is indeed all, for the world to know
When expressed in everything we are
In everything we do and say
Every human heart and soul united
For the one glorious cause to be displayed

The former understanding of each and every soul
The dense mist seeming a reality
The human senses surrounded in fog
With love and in us all
The dense mist will disappear
Radiant sunshine penetrating from above

The struggles in life will take care of themselves
In love's reflection and with faith, they are gently erased
Around the world, the few are becoming many
In peaceful and quiet understanding
Around the world, love being expressed
Many beautiful radiant explosions

Man will at last achieve his birthright
The true reflection he is meant to manifest
Love of one another in tenderness expressed
Oh, how grateful we should all become
How we will all indeed be truly blessed

Evil influences at last pushed aside
Disappearing as the dense fog evaporates
To nevermore cloud the minds and hearts of mankind
Overcome at last, the sun bursting forth
Warm rays of love to all
Harmony—the Creator's blessing

    I was sitting by water's edge and watching a dense fog creep slowly over islands and the sea, obliterating everything from sight. This writing came about as the sun's warmth at last made the fog and mist vanish and once again exposed the truth of what was there, and oh-so beautiful.

Dethroning God

As I go through each day observing what is going on
There seems to be such a movement now
Subtle things said, written, or placed before us
The movement takes on trying to dethrone God

Many are aware of this, even though subtly presented
We must all be cognizant of this darker presence
It is cunning, crafty, and it is slithering into our lives by various means
And the serpent gets bolder as times goes on

No part of the world in which we live
Seems to be protected from this
There is upheaval almost everywhere, it seems
Country against country, people and their beliefs being trampled

The political arena having twists and turns
The rights of many seem to be in violation of others
So much unrest, and where will it end?
Tolerance, patience, and understanding of each other, a start

For those of us who believe in God, a creator of us all
Even called Father, the Light, or some other name
Can we not then finally unite mankind?
And at least accept one another, each having a right

I, for one, do not wish to see my God dethroned
The divine essence of all life under attack
If one does not believe, then fine
But at least can we try to love one another more?

Doorknobs

While visiting a friend one afternoon
And viewing some of his doorknob collection
My thoughts drifted toward the Divine premise
That we are provided special doorknobs in life
And each one opening a door from God

Each presented door is unique
And one of a kind toward an ultimate goal
Behind each one another step forward
Another blessing to yet unfold
To and for our ultimate calling
After all, He already knows

As each doorknob is utilized
Having the faith it has been provided to us
Each door then gently pushed open
Behind each one a new beginning
Oh, the glory and power presented

To fulfill and bless each of us
A demonstration of His love truly given
For all to embrace tenderly
From each heart and soul
The magnificent recognition

The human trick becomes, however
In listening to the still, quiet voice
To have the human courage, wisdom
To turn the doorknob in the first place
Each one that He has lovingly provided

But in having total faith
In the Father/Creator of us all
The quiet messages received
We are presented a doorknob to use
So use them one and all

The doors will then open
In the correct order as presented
Then, each doorknob becomes
Even more cherished and beautiful
And the correct and fruitful results attained

While visiting the musician David Templeton in Seattle, I was able to view part of his beautiful private collection, and from that, this writing transpired as I thought about doorknobs in relation to the Divine presence. And so the creative spirit can flow in a very positive manner, as it does in God, with our allowance continually to us.

Dry Sand

Dry sand, so hard to walk on
We sink, slip, toil, and stumble
Our legs struggle to keep pushing
Our feet tire easily from onward motion

It would be so much nicer, we think
The sand moistened with water
It would certainly make our traction
So much easier and for us to make headway

Our legs would not have to work so hard
It would alleviate using so much mortal energy
I wonder about the challenge of our forward motion
Easier is not always better or the purpose

In life through our human journey
We must all go without once in a while
The moisture, the water on the dry sand
In making our forward progress last

As I recall "Footsteps in the Sand"
There was no easy base on which to walk
Jesus's footsteps carrying us are deep
Sometimes heavy burdens put onto his shoulders

We at times never know them
He has taken them on himself
For us to be free for a little while
Oh, thank you, Son of God

Just think of how many He has done this for
How many burdens He has carried
His shoulders, legs, and feet must be oh-so weary
We all must become so very grateful

I know, however, that by His large capacity to love us
He does not consider it weary work
He is not tired of the toil and is not strained
His teardrops of compassion falling on the dry sand
Make his journey for us less tedious

Let us all be so thankful for Him
His never-ending footprints digging into the sand
Lifting and carrying some of our burdens for us
Eternally grateful we should all be
For the Savior, Son of God, we thank Thee

Dust Your Britches Off

It is so easy for us all to spiral downward
When we stumble and allow ourselves to fall
Depending upon how we fall or just slide
We may want to stay there and give up

We may find comfort just being down and out
Even though perhaps pain, sorrow, tears come
But then there comes a time when we get tired of them
The feelings of decaying not our true purpose

Pick yourself up, as I have to do at times myself
Stand erect and take your true place once again
Dust those britches off, say a prayer and then "Amen"
Life is too short and our place not to be on the ground

Get rid of the dirt, dust, and make yourself clean again
Know where your true strength comes from
You have it within you from which to draw
No matter what the circumstances seem to be

It is our right to be happy, whole, and complete
To feel all the wonderful things we have been given
Life, truth, and love from above, the constant
Dust yourself off, stand upright, and be all you can be

Overcome the dust; now let us all just do it

Dwell in the Silence of Sweet Healing

Even though the journey, at times, holds turbulence
For the heart and soul and your inner core
You feel inwardly dashed upon the rocks
Know that there is no desertion by the Lord

He came to save, forgive our sins
He came to teach, to nourish and show the way
No matter at what point mortally you are
Know full well He forgives and allows you to go on

Repent for the past aggressions with sincerity
Not only upon others but yourself as well
Allow the forgiveness from Him to flow upon you
Then be free to climb upward and onward

In spite of what you may believe
There is no time frame set upon you
But as you come to the known crossroads
Seek, find, and become released from self-bondage

There is always a mortal marked time
When decisions need to be focused on
Then, yes, all need to turn around
And, in doing so, look inwardly to your inner depths

He knows each heart and soul
Our Creator is all love for all time
And in being that, there is no negative power
Thus, He does not abandon you, even in your mortal hours

Rise up human being and stand erect in presence
Fling your positive energy out to the galaxies and beyond
He surrounds all, as He is everywhere
Love, sweet love is so very patient with you

Even though the exterior of the human
Can portray on-guard, self-protecting aura
As you seek the soft and loving highest Divine power
You can all continue the work and even let go of guilt

Each step forward is a victory
Not only for you but also for Him
Let His magnification sweetly embrace and heal wounds
He loves you, child of God, as He waits most patiently on you

Climb the mountains with firm steps forward
Take a hold of His loving extended hand
He is always ready and waits upon you, the mortal
The forgiveness already given, so claim it

Thank Him and then keep progressing with forward motion
Each positive step of even realization a plus
Each repentant event taken may not be the end
But each one overcome provides healing and renewal

Then take each lesson, self-realization, and allow self-forgiveness

This writing was inspired by a Chippewa warrior very dear to me in making a comment that he feared God was about to abandon him—that mortal time might be running out for God's understanding and patience—as the man's mortal journey continued. Each of us, during our mortal time here on Mother Earth, comes repeatedly to the same crossroad. When the time finally arrives, and seeking God's help, we then turn our situations around and rectify what we may be doing incorrectly. It is also important we allow the self-forgiveness needed as He forgives us when we sincerely ask and truly know and understand He never abandons because Divine love continues for all time.

Each Day a Precious Gift

How many days I have wasted; I have lost count
How many opportunities did I not embrace?
They may have been gently placed before me
But, I chose not to listen or dismissed them

The feeling of not wanting to go into unknown waters
To have gone beyond my personal comfort zones
To have stepped outside my enclosed limited mental box
How many more blessings would have come my way?

When I was younger, yes, so stubborn was I
I knew better, of course, and oh, how I was proven wrong
My arrogance in thinking, I knew it all then
Now my human time longer traveled, as I look back

Yes, I did not always make the correct decisions
Either in choosing people to be in my life
Or in doing or saying certain things to others
I now ask God's forgiveness as a child to a parent

How does the saying go that I have heard?
Oh yes, I remember it now thinking back
"If only I knew then what I do now"
Hindsight is such a curse or blessing in remembering

Of course, we cannot know all the answers, even now
To what we have to encounter and decisions to make
The journey, the different paths we all go on
Everyone has to take the walk in life and learn

When younger, we dismiss human time so readily
We think we are invincible, so many more years ahead
But, as time marches on, we discover at some point
Guess again, each day then accumulates one after the other

I wish I had treasured each day I had been given
When younger and not dismissed so readily in haste
The lesson learned, over human marked time, as I grow older
Life, each day, such a precious gift to have and treasure

I will be so much more grateful now for each one
Even though I may relax now and then, and that is okay
I will think of days like that as a precious gift as well
To be able to energize myself for another blessed given day

EMERGENCE

For so many years
In a cocoon was I
Wrapped up tightly
Comfortable—seeming delight

The events through life
Struggles but also joys
Safely hidden away
My eyes closed

Then an event
Taking place somewhat unexpectedly
The emergence, the awakening
Freedom—flight

The cocoon left behind
Wings outstretched
A butterfly now formed
On the airways from Heaven

A new inward light rekindled
A new outward appearance too
The feeling of beauty and peace
United with serenity

As I go onward
My dreams so impassioned
The feelings of anticipation
The thrill of revelations

EMPOWERED

In the still quiet moments, I go to God
Praying to be guided and protected with His grace
To do His will, not mine, while here on Earth
To radiate His gentle and loving ways to others

Each day so important to quietly commune
No matter how busy I am during my day
There are many moments that I can and should
Declare His love and ask to listen and obey

I feel so blessed that at last I understand more
There were many times that I would and then did not
I still search for answers to my questions, of course
I feel grateful, though, that I even want to learn more

When I make the effort, go to Him, and push me aside
In completely letting go and with love in my heart
Knowing where my true strength comes from
Sometimes mortal inclinations can try to get in the way

When this happens and I do not feel empowered
By the grace of the Father/Creator of us all
I feel empty inside and a void, uncertainty, even panic
Then I remind myself not to try to go on the journey alone

Human will pushed aside the best I can accomplish
When I try genuinely to let go, let God manifest unto me
I can almost sense His smile back to me; but a child I am
At least I am trying harder now, and He knows

It sometimes is a daily struggle to stay on the right course
Every time I make the attempt and at least try
Things open up for me in demonstration, peace
I feel more empowered by the Divine connection

Faith, Hope, and Belief

As a child, I was taught many things
Some elements I did absorb even then
From the basics presented, from the Sunday school I attended
The stories brought forth from the book called the Bible

As I grew from being a child into an adult—or was I?
I did not always apply the teachings I had learned
But when things got rough, I recalled the principles
And leaned upon my Father in Heaven once again

I, at times, would simply just declare in earnest
"His love directs; His love protects me all the while"
As I remember my mortal mother teaching me
A simple declaration from faith, hope, and belief

I, many times, would allow things and others to enter
My life, my circumstances; then would manifest
Mortal difficulties—"Now I have another mess"
Then drawing, once again, the Divine more into things

I have come full circle now, brought back to Him, as a child
In quietly and firmly placing God/Creator first, foremost
Now I cling to my ultimate Father in Heaven
For my direction, protection, and greater understanding

From His love, all things flow to every human being
When I let go, let God truly be in my thoughts
The mortal mental battles intrude, unyielding pursuit of me, at times
But I continually reverse seeming negatives back to Him

I am so much more at peace now clinging to Him
It is now deeply felt within my very inner core and being
I have learned through mortal life and triumphs
That I will always keep alive in my consciousness
Faith, hope, and belief nurtured from above

False Fear Overcome

How many times do we need to learn, oh Father of us all?
In this human journey of ours, as ever onward we go
False fears preventing so many times for each one
Overwhelming us, the shadows, the mist interrupting
Covering up the clear and resounding true brilliant light

We all have different fears that come into our lives
The human mind carries on the battle within
We can become terrified of them as they occur
They try to engulf, and we allow them reality

We need to all be on our guard, ever diligent
No matter what form they present themselves
Our hesitation to totally embrace and fight against them
But we all must take our mental and birthright stand

It is our right to be free from false fears that we impose
To totally let go, let God/Source be in control
We need in calm reflection and in going to Him
Declare we, and also others, are His reflection in pure light

In this perfect reflection from the ultimate Source
In our declarations and total belief and faith
Nothing but good, God/Source is truly our right
In true manifestation, we then overcome and go on

We must cling tightly to our true Light, our Source for all good
It is our right to have the beautiful reflection
The true Light is brilliant and true in perfection
In complete wholeness, ours to behold and radiate

We must ever be on our human guard
The human battles of the mind must all be won
But, in this reflection of the great I Am
All can be attained and truly our right to demonstrate

Feather Cloud

It was a beautiful warm summer day, soft breeze present
As we gathered and banded together to relish in the event
On the shore, next to the sea so calm, native boats, procession
We were waiting for them to arrive from Alaska

They had come so very far already with determination
Performing the old ways of their forefathers
Paying tribute and honor to their fellow brothers, sisters
To share the stories and music of the ancients to keep alive

As the boats came to shore, oars upright in salute
The chants, greetings given and received in the old way
Blessing one another, sea to sky, Mother Earth, mankind
Homage was indeed paid by all with love in their hearts

Music and dances were performed, the ways remembered
Ritualistic costumes and colors were displayed
Various tribes became one in unison with all others
Telling, sharing of all, remembering the ancient ones

There was laughter in the air, the smells of food prepared
As all mingled together for one cause, and abundant smiles
Tribute, honor, sharing, and love pronounced to each other and all
It was truly such a fulfilling, beautiful, and wonderful day

As we departed when it was time to go
Walking back to our vehicle, safe transportation home
We looked up into the blue sky above, "Oh my"
My heart soared as to what was provided for the day

As the positive energy from all filled the air
A single cloud appeared overhead, breathtaking
I just smiled, took my picture, and understood
Oh, native feather cloud in the sky, you represented so much

FEELING LOST

Depending upon our individual life occurrences
By chance or chosen determinations made
At times, we all feel lost on the journey
There are many questions from us all
Are we making the correct choices?

Why do we feel lost at times?
We all need to know our true Guide
He, our Creator, is at the front of the line
The torch always brightly illuminating our path

We must have our eyes opened, to go in faith
In order to recognize and see the true light
The illumination and direction from our Creator
The paths clearly brightened for all of us

We need to gather our inner strength and peace
Declare our oneness with Him all of the time
Each day in thankfulness and true gratefulness
Declare that to Him, the Divine presence

No matter what the human strife seems to be
We each encounter, as our journey progresses
And know full well the light shines brightly
For us and for all of mankind as well

Come to Him, our Creator, with true emotion
With gratefulness in your heart and soul expressed
And with possessing resolute faith, we are never really lost
We are one with Him, the Father of us all, ever-present

DARA MARIE

Fire Ceremony: Spiritual Journey on Sugar Beach

We gathered together, a circle we did make
Praying in declaration our oneness to the Divine
On Sugar Beach, Maui, we were united
Oh, what a spiritual place to be for this first time

We called upon all the Divine oracles
Deeper and deeper did we go to the source of all
Each one in quiet abandonment, reaching for the stars
We let go of mortal thoughts as we continued on

Pressing ourselves forward in and with presence
To the oneness of each soul, reaching attainment
In receivership, we all became absorbed in peaceful bliss
The circle becoming ever stronger, oh, the energy

With soft and tender voice, we were led
Propelling each of us beyond ourselves
The Divine presence talking softly to each one
Peace and harmony was being felt by all

Each had a journey of fulfillment and dedication
As the circle expanded in thought, perception
Listening to the waves gently coming ashore
While sitting quietly, in unison, on Sugar Beach, Maui

Energy released as well as received
My fingers began to tingle and vibrate for some time
I found myself concentrating on them as the energy increased
I knew and just smiled, as I understood the meaning

It was a confirmation to and for me from this union
The release of my creativity through my hands
Others experienced their own journey they needed
We embraced the meaning of it all and just gently smiled

As I floated upward with mind and soul
Reaching to the stars and well beyond
Extending my love onward and in appreciation
To what was happening on this beautiful ground

I realize I can do this on my own
Each human being can if he or she wishes
Total release of one's self to the Higher Power
But, oh, what a special place in which to accomplish

I found myself pushing my toes into the buttery-like sand
So soft it is, and I treasure the experience
As I mentally came down to earthly plane once more
I looked up to the beautiful stars; silence except the sea

I had to write of this experience
To touch base with my senses while still fresh
To once again read this work, close my eyes
And pull from memory the sacred ceremony

To once again truly feel my first experience of this
As I climbed upward and beyond with my whole being
Nothing will ever replace, though, this first encounter
On the beautiful soft sugar beach in Maui

Fixing It

She typed, "I don't know how to fix it"
Calling for help in order to combat mortal manifestation
I found myself automatically typing back to her
Draw more upon the Divine well
As you ask, you shall receive the answers
In and for what you need first to fix it as you say

So many times, we all cannot clearly see
Even in having the spiritual connection in place
We need to all step back from self, I as well
Realize the Divine well to draw upon is very deep
The first step in overcoming whatever presented
Lies in asking to receive mortally what we need for reversal

We can help others, as I tried to lovingly accomplish
Now I have the challenge of it myself from my response
In typing something to and for another
With loving support, the pure intention
Now I must further that in and for my own mortal living
I must also take my words and, with resolve, embrace them

We need to, I think, be quieted first with thoughts and emotions
Then as we declare our oneness with the Divine and receive
We need also to understand we do not need to fix anything
But our Father will give us the tools to challenge whatever
Whether understanding, resolve, courage, strength, it does not matter
What we each lack in mortally overcoming something can then be supplied

Yes, we as mortals need to do certain things, of course
Action and perceptions of thought so important
To lay the basic foundation down mentally
And in doing so, allow God to work and provide direction
Or, whatever we need to be able to combat the other forces
In order to know then how to overcome and receive the rightful answers

As soon as I had typed the response to her
I realized I must apply the same principles for me
In trying to pass on love and give a supportive hand
If we are in truth mode for ourselves, it comes back to us as well
The message loud and clearly brought forward for me
In giving, so we can receive back for our own journey

None of us is immune from the promise of elevated thinking
We all have our own growth to achieve and time frame
In giving someone else my answer, my response
I automatically received one back for me to dwell on
Now I have to use that as a tool itself for progress
As I climb my own mountains, one step at a time

We have faith, hope, and belief to draw upon
Let us all go forward toward the Supreme Light
And, as we ask our Father in quiet abandonment
To guide and direct us through the Divine way
Supply our mortal presence with what each may need
To calm, to support, to provide us the tools to overcome

He already knows the answers to what each needs
We as mortal beings need to direct the mind to the Supreme Source
We also have to be willing, however, to truly let go, let God
In doing this, we can ask for help in reversing and not fixing it
Then we have the tools needed to succeed and claim victory
As each step forward is taken, we continue to climb our mountains

From false perceptions that others may try to perpetuate
Or circumstances we ourselves have allowed to happen
There is always an answer, a solution
To and for every mortal burden that would seem to overtake us
At times even a mortal gulp necessary, as we continue on
With each progressive step, mortal gains are made

Having Him provide perhaps the courage, strength alone is much
The resolve to change this or that in our lives
As some point, though, we have to step up to the plate
And, yes, do our own work for resolution of each problem
All can be accomplished with what He gives us inside
The nourishment needed for each soul toward victory

How wonderful it is to absolutely believe and know
We have Him on our side at all times
For whatever we humanly may lack in order to claim the victory
We then go onward and are able to cope with anything
He provides the needed elements for us to conquer our challenges
Yes, we then surely claim our rightful spiritual victory over mortal
        circumstances

Free will of thought, elevation, He gives to us all
Now let us pray for strength, guidance, and protection
In allowing our Father to fulfill that promise for us
We can fix anything, overcome with the Divine
Even mortal healing, whatever it may be, can be attained
Thus the promise given and demonstrated long ago

So, I will not try from now on to fix anything
Without going to my true Source of all things
He will give me the tools to combat my challenges, large or small
Whatever I may lack, I pray for Him to supply these things
Then when I quietly listen and receive what is needed
I am equipped with the missing elements to claim my victory

One step at a time, overcome and mend what needs to be fixed
No matter what it is, you can and will with your Father
With faith, hope, and placing yourself in His tender care
He will show you how, where, why, and provide the inner calm
He also will provide what you might not even know is lacking
Remember, He knows already, and so we ask first for that blessing

We first step aside and ask Him into our heart, our mortal mind
The next steps will then be much easier, calmer
As we will have the knowledge and understanding
From the total release to Him, the supply given to us
Instead of us saying, "I don't know how to fix it"
We should say something like, "Father, please supply me what I need
With You at my side, I will then have the power to correct it"

Forward Motion

In looking to the future days of my human existence
Why, oh why, am I hesitant so many times?
I sometimes feel the knot inside of me, deep within
I wish that it could just be untied and released

I close my eyes while listening to calming music
It helps bring me to a peaceful place deep within
To commune and connect to the great I Am
My mind slowly becomes calmer once again

The past I understand more, of course
It has already happened and is familiar to me
Decisions made, joy or sadness expressed
Now I look to an uncertain, unknown future

Many lessons have been learned, I hope
There were many times I stumbled or fell
I do not want to repeat the mistakes of the past
But I do wish to embrace waiting love and joy

One thing I have learned over human time
Each moment I put the Creator of us all in control
Going to the Divine and letting go of human will
I have been blessed more than I could ever know

I rest my weary mind, as the soothing music flows
Making the connection with love from above
When I place myself with Him for all things
My forward motion will be full of promise

Someday, I will look back upon this time
A soft gentle smile on my face, the realization
That what I was concerned about now never happened
With Him at my side, connecting to the all-knowing

Forward motion of Divine Life brought me to where I am now

The Four Seasons of Life

Spring
We come into this world
A new bud having been created
Pure in heart, pure in spirit
A new life yet to be unfolded
Existence in human form
To grow, to become as beautiful as we can become

Summer
Warmth and further growth's potential
The full blossom being extended by a stronger stem
Nurtured by the sun and needing the water of life
The beauty within us to nourish and give joy to others
To reflect all we can be, beauty from within

Fall
This season represents our withdrawal
We, as human beings, sometimes experience
The cooling down, the clouds hiding the sun
Our understanding and closeness to the One
The sustenance provided from above

Winter
Because of human will, the cold blasts of life may occur
Pounding at our hearts, our true being
The storm with anger and waves attempting to consume us
Trying to push us downward and drown us
But with persistence and faith, we can all tread and keep afloat

Spring Again
It returns once more with the promise of renewal
The bud reaching for the nourishing light; the new beginning
Ever onward, we advance toward further growth
Extending, reaching toward the sun, the warmth
The promise of this renewal once again
The beauty of each soul to be reflected
The true and promised fulfillment of man

Free Flight of Imagination

Imagination, what a wonderful and glorious thing
Fed and released to the inner soul of each one
Nourished by the lullaby of angels, surrendering mortal inhibitions
All we have to do is allow it to take flight

As a bird that glides on the airways
Heaven bound and free just to be
To let the mind take its flight and direction
Oh, what a wonderful thing indeed

To sit quietly in a comfortable chair, perhaps
To have the right music flowing through the silence
The eyes close, sweet bliss of heart and soul
The mind in peaceful presence can then pour forth

The senses are renewed and even awakened
Many things can be then presented to each
People, places, and things beyond our own mortality
Flow freely to each, the beautiful connection made

One can drift with the clouds and be with the angels
Be in places yet unseen but envisioned
Concepts can be formed and come into reality
Thoughts divine, another plateau reached

We all can do this, each to receive enrichment
What is needed can appear and nourish
If nothing else is gained from the exercise
We can at least achieve a level of peaceful contentment

Drift away where you need to go and mentally fly
Embrace what you are surely told and given
As a bird, wings spread on the sea of air
Let the imagination be released in peace and solitude

We can all be surprised, at times, as we let it transpire
Where this may take us, a possible new journey
Renewal, growth, nourishment, peace
The time well worth allowing flight of imagination

Since being an only child, my imagination technique transpired from an early age and without listening to music. Now, I use the beautiful music that is offered by many to help and release my heart and soul with abandonment of the mortal senses, and I can make the total-surrender jump to receive quite easily, and to receive from the Divine realm, as well. Music is not always needed for this process, however. You have to push out of the mind completely anything of the world and focus to receive the blessings that God, the All-knowing, has in store for you or even for others.

Take the time, make the effort, and great things can and will happen to you, as everyone has this capability. But few will go there as they either fear results, cannot totally let go of presupposed mortal boundaries, or do not even wish to try. It can be done with patience, perseverance, and belief. Always remain in gratefulness when you receive, and if what comes is indeed from the Divine realm, there will never be any doubt from whence it came. You will automatically just know. Always remain with your Divine channel connection as purely as you can have it, and remain with and in the Love Supreme.

Free Ride, Transportation Provided

Free ride provided on my log in the ocean, as I rest my weary wings
How nice to find it, to just be in peace, riding the current
To have movement not really knowing where it will take me
I, as a bird, can watch the beauty unfold before me

Peace, tranquility, beauty, and yes, human beings
One is taking my picture now, as I take my ride with the flow
I hope they understand the total concept of it all
Even a bird like me gets it, natural instinct provided

God/Creator has given me so much in my form
Even though a bird, I have a brain and perceptions
I have natural instincts within me, just like humans
I hope the human beings can embrace this also

I am not the prettiest bird around by any means
But as I sit here on this log, provided for me
I feel proud of what I am and my worthiness
I do hope the human beings also understand

Oh yes, I see much beauty of our world around me
I embrace so much of what our Creator has done
I may be just a bird to you human beings
But my head is held up high

I have my place in the total scope of things
I have my own worth and things to do
We all were created for a specific purpose
Our Creator surely knows what he has done

As these human beings watch me float by
On my log that was provided for me to rest and be
I hope they too will avail themselves of this
The log, our Creator's, the great I Am's, transportation

While walking the beach where I lived in Anacortes, Washington, a friend of mine saw this bird perched on a log floating and drifting on the currents in front of us. It continued on with its free transportation until it disappeared out of sight. Thus, this writing came into being, and of course, I drew from the spiritual realm, which has become second nature to me in and with my thoughts and perceptions.

Freedom of Another Place, Another Time

The music takes me beyond myself
I close my eyes and drift calmly away
To another place, another time dimension
The freedom to experience things, some not yet reality

I visit paths in a deep-green, lush forest
The smells of sweetness permeate the air
Peace, calm, and tranquility are mine
A rainforest, tall trees, green lace hanging down

Now I drift out to sea in a small sailboat
On calm blue waters towards the horizon
Small islands now and then appear
The cares of the world are left behind, freedom

Another journey along cobblestoned streets
Of some ancient city or town, times that are gone
Small shops to visit, architecture to absorb
Greeting gentle people I do not know with love

Now I am in a green meadow somewhere
A pond and small waterfall gently cascading
I sit quietly by its side; peace and contentment are mine
Small creatures come to drink; I just quietly watch

I now can go anywhere I want to in my mind
In letting the imagination gently release self
Years, centuries even, are brought forward
As the mind, senses, emotions float and soar

I do this when escape from worldly cares are needed
It renews my soul, nourishes and enriches me
As I drift up to the clouds, perhaps, and back again
I almost hate the return to reality from beyond
Another place, another time, I will allow myself complete freedom

This poem was inspired from Yanni's *Reflections of Passion* CD.

From Your Love, Your Son

In quiet faith we go on our mortal journey
Apprehensions must be put aside
We know our Father, Creator, God
Is always at our side

We reach our hand upward
For Him to lovingly hold onto
Gently and tenderly guiding us
Our path, at times, unknown

We should pray every day
To retain our elevated thinking
We can pause and quiet our minds
With confidence, serenely listen

Please direct us in Your way
Let us reflect You in all things
Give us, please, what we need
To accomplish Your directives

A child of You, the Most High, we all are
All should declare continuously
Let the child be obedient
To our Father, to His throne

You gave us Your Son
To show us the elevated Divine way
He humanly endured so much
For us to be redeemed

He was lovingly given to us
That we may see the light
When we travel toward it
Oh, how beautiful the journey
How straight then the path

With grateful hearts
With reverence and humility
We all must go on our own way
On our own road to our destiny

In love we all should be
Of the sacrifice made for us
Your Son given so that we may have sight
Clarity, and understanding of your kingdom
From Your love for all mankind

FRUIT SALAD

It comes to mind when preparing a salad
Oh, how divine the recipe has become
A fruit salad with different ingredients
It incorporates many colors and tastes

The recipe wisely calling for this and that
All carefully placed and blended together
Each ingredient bringing out various flavors
In unison and complementing one another

Then each ingredient is carefully mixed all together
Gently trying not to bruise or hurt each one
Each separate element being important
In order to accomplish the final result

In looking at the total recipe for mankind
How our Creator has done this so well
Each separate heritage important on its own
To achieve the final beautiful mixture

Now if the final mixed ingredients
Could, at last, come together
Embracing love, tolerance, peace, and joy
The end result could be so very beautiful

DARA MARIE

The Game of Slip and Slide

We can all pass messages, our experiences onward
In order to try to help others through love
But in doing so, we can also permit something
We can start to lose focus for ourselves in the process

Yes, we all can receive messages for others
From the divine connection or from our own experiences
There are times, however, when we all, myself included, must
Not forget what we ourselves have to work on

Looking inwardly without predefined thought
Clearly delving into what we ourselves are permitting
We all have our own things to overcome, upward the climb
The other side still tries to captivate us and bind up firmly

We are so intent on lovingly trying to help others
And in pure love and intention from us to them
Give them encouragement, examples of what we conquered
But then, there is always more we ourselves are presented with

We do not have the right to judge others as they struggle onward
To capture more of the divine influence for themselves
In their own circumstances to gain a stronger foothold
We need also to look inwardly and handle our own things
We have our own valleys, foothills, and mountains to ascend

To ever climb upward to our Source we believe in
To break out of our own clouded understanding
Sometimes it is a slip-and-slide motion on the journey
We must all push ourselves up again, however
And continue the forward motion, which should be our direction

We need to pause, though, once in a while, as well
And through introspection and attempting to be honest
We can have an understanding of where others are
But by being truly honest and open with ourselves
We realize that so many are ahead of us in areas we are not

Each person has the right of greater attainment
To be truly blessed and conquer whatever his or her needs are
Regardless of what we have allowed ourselves to do and become
Once in a while, we slip and slide, which is good in a way
It just points us in the right direction and to further growth

On and on it goes for us all, as we continue to try to climb
One of the keys, I think anyway, in conquering
Is being very honest with our inner core, our soul
And with this key be better than we were yesterday

We are all given free will, choices that we possess
To make the decisions that determine our life's directions
The slip-and-slide method does have its own value
But, here again, we all need to be awakened

Sometimes revelations come like a bolt of lightning
Other times from others lovingly passing on their own to us
The quiet, still voice we can hear again if we allow it
Is always guiding and trying to talk to us

We know deep within ourselves, the inner core
Whether we are doing something we should not
It nags at our being, through our human mind
Telling us God knows better, "Now quit slipping and sliding
Pick yourself up and gain strength; go onward"

Many times we still humanly struggle with this and that
In not really wanting even to start the correction
Ah, we are all the same in so many things of mortal life
I myself need to start some things in earnest, always a challenge
"Oh, my Source, my God, give me the strength needed"

Why do we fight it so often—our human stubbornness, perhaps?
When overcoming what we need to accomplish
The other side, often by our own thinking and perception
Would so love to keep us as the captive, imprisoned

The true test for each of us as a human being, myself included
With my own things to overcome and demonstrate for me
Is first asking for the help and then trying to really listen
The game of slip and slide is not really fun for anyone

Human choices, however, are always such a factor
We at times need to really and finally decide for ourselves
Once and for all, we can and need to say firmly, "Enough is enough"
Then we can pick our feet up and advance upward and onward

Time after time, we all go through this slip-and-slide routine
Others have conquered some things we now struggle with
But in allowing others who have gone before us in some things
And in going to the Ultimate, the Supreme, the Source for all
We each can and will overcome what we need to have done

There will always be more things to learn and perceive
It never seems finally to be concluded here and in this form
But, at the same time, how boring it would become
For us to be absolutely perfect in every way while here
I know just one; the Ultimate Source is the Father of us all

If we give up and throw our hands in the air in disgust
Declaring sometimes, "I do not want to fight anymore" or
"It is too much for me to go on, and I am weakened"
Then we will just slide backwards once again even more
We deprive ourselves so much more in life, our right to have

Why, oh why are we so stubborn so many times?
I have been there myself and continue in some things
I guess we all have to learn more from the end result
All in order to make us humanly better, more in perfection
That is the greatest challenge before each of us

I'm getting tired of the slip-and-slide game for me
But I refuse to give up for myself, as well as for others
I need to love myself more, I guess, as I love them
I, then, in writing this have helped even me, the release
I will work harder against the slip and slide I permit

Humility needed as forward progress is attained for us all

    I have been honored and blessed in being of help to others who have been to the depths of despair and many who were encountering things that I had already gone through. I have also had my own challenges, and thus this writing came about when I was permitting myself to feel down over something that I felt missing in my life. As one continues on the upward journey, and with having humbleness in place, even when we can help others, we learn that the slip-and-slide factor of our mortal existence happens to us all. Each time we reverse it, the blessings of being resolute in going forward and not backwards truly does manifest, as we continue to put our faith with our Supreme Father, and as children, we also continue to learn and grow stronger.

Gentle and Loving Extended Hand

We met one afternoon to share a dream of yours
The dream of a material structure, sitting on sacred ground
I relished in seeing it because I truly wanted to share it with you
Dreams shared between two who truly care for one another

We had to go down a steep winding trail, and on and on it did go
To reach the beach, quite the journey I must say
But the destination worth the effort in just going for it
Many things to embrace, the calming presence among the trees

The trail downward, slick from fallen leaves, somewhat treacherous
I was somewhat hesitant at the time, now upon peaceful reflection
You went before me, offering your hand, no fearful thought
To help steady, protect, and guide me, as I made my way

The thoughts come back to me clearly and now expand
Of how our Creator gives us His assistance as well
Lovingly offered, always at the ready for us all
As we reach for His hand, it is offered for what is needed

With gratefulness in my heart for your loving hand
I had complete trust we would not slip or slide into harm
We both could have easily lost our footing and tumbled downward
But in total faith and belief, we were both taken care of

I could not go back up the hill very well, my energy was depleted
You could, but I did worry, as darkness quickly approached
I put you with Him and knew full well in declaration
His hand of protection and guiding existed, and it was declared

Down the beach I walked and patiently waited for your return
You then got the car and came back for me via another route
The path for retrieving me now blocked, and darkness was upon us
We each decided to hoof it and eventually met up once again

Off we did go, climbing up another hill, to the waiting car
I took your arm this time, as I was getting somewhat tired
You might have been as well, but steadily upward we walked
Kind of reminds me of our journey with Him, but He never is weary

We both shared a most treasured part of a day
And the memory will always last for me
As you reached out your hand to protect, steady, and guide
I will always remember that His hand is there as well

It is always extended to us from Him
As mine is always given in return to you
We help one another in quiet surrender of self
The helping hand extended through loving ways

Let me remember, try to do the same for others
As you lovingly extended your hand to mine
As He provides to all that would reach for it
To help steady, guide, and protect through love

GOD'S GIFT: MY DAUGHTER, KIMBERLY LORRAINE

Some years ago, I gave birth
Oh beautiful bundle of joy
So small you were, so pink, so pretty

I marveled at this gift God had given
How delicate you were
Your tiny features, oh-so perfect

I thanked Him for my perfect gift
So wonderful you were
You shivered, shook; you fussed
Until you were wrapped and surrounded in cloth

You grew and grew
Toddler of mine
Your first steps, smiles
Oh, how divine

You continued on
Many endeavors
Some in triumph
Some heartache too
But overcoming all

When you fell
Picking yourself up
Determination galore
You knew not then
His loving arms
Encircled you evermore

As you journeyed
Through our human existence
The straight, the narrow
The curved and twisted paths
He was always near
To love, to embrace

With abundant patience
As you weaved your way
Through human decisions
Some good, some bad
He always brought your focus back

His protection and direction
Always picking you up
The twisted path no more
Your footsteps steady
On the right course

Oh beautiful, oh wonderful gift
From God you came to me
A mother to teach
Oh, but a mother to learn
I thank Him for thee

So proud, I am, of the woman you have become
The flower, perfect petals
Nourished from the sun
Heaven's light you have absorbed
Blossoming with such beauty galore

A tender heart
A tender soul

You have become a mother of two girls
Each unique in her own way
Loving each from God
Guiding, prodding, watching
Both going on their own path

As I watch in wonderment
Your accomplishments so many
The flower continues to grow
Each petal searching and reaching for the sun
Oh, please continue to grow

The light of God continues to nourish
The stem is strong, upright, and straight
The center core is firm
A mother's pride
A mother's love
Her beautiful unfolding loving flower

Oh, what can I say?
What can I do?
Continue on with His love and sunshine
Continue to grow, my beautiful daughter
Oh, my beautiful flower

When you think of me after I'm gone
This human form no more
To be with our Father, God
In loving arms I will be forevermore

Smile and know that I am always near
The sunshine, the rain
Touching your heart, touching your soul
Nourishing the beautiful flower again

And, when we meet again
In love united, in Heaven's place
My arms outstretched to you
We will both know that we have indeed been renewed

Our journey continues
In and with God's Love
Renewal uniting us once more
Both of us His flowers
Upright to the sun
The light of Him
Life for evermore

I know not for certain
What the next journey will be
But in faith we will go
To the next level, to the next step
Oh how exciting it will be

What we have not overcome while here
We will surely know
His loving arms encircling us
What will be, will be

You were God's first thought and creation
I was then blessed giving you birth
Receiving such joy then and now
You are not only my daughter
You are now my best friend

GOD'S PERFECT REFLECTION

If you are troubled and face a life crisis
Know where your true life is
Not in this mortal form
But always with God, the Creator

Pay homage and declare your love for Him
Ask for His help and blessing
Truly believe you are His reflection
Perfect in every way

Overcome your fear; it may be false anyway
Ask for His healing revelations
The comfort given like no other
Here again, God's reflective grace

Our Father, Omnipresence Supreme
Is always here with us
It is not a dream
His love expressed to us
Hold on to His comforting embrace

Truly believe all things can be
With Him and from His love
Mortal human anguish overcome
You are His beautiful reflection
Oh child of God

Each one of us a child of the Most High
He encircles us with His loving embrace
We have not been abandoned
He sometimes has, though, by us

Know your rightful place
Protected and kept under His loving care
Let not evil influence creep into your thoughts
Leaving your mind full of fear

Continually declare the positives through prayer
His reflection, perfect in every way
Lovingly given, lovingly and gratefully receiving it
Declare yourself one with Him

His perfect, beautiful, and whole reflection

God's Tears

I once felt ashamed
Tears falling from my eyes
Running and escaping down my cheek
Oh, what is the matter with me?

The heart hurting so
The feeling of despair
Oh dear Lord, where are You?
Please comfort me once again

I then discovered I am not the only one
I am no longer ashamed
We all do it from time to time
The feeling of release from the pain

I wonder if God cries
When His children, His reflections of love
Are disobedient to His kingdom
Oh, His despair

I fantasize His tears
Raindrops falling from the sky
I do not mind any longer
Either from joy or sadness

It would be even sadder indeed
If I could not have the emotions to release
Those tears are meant for inward healing
Or for the joys in life . . . rejoice

GOOD GRIEF, THE TRAFFIC

When we wake from our slumber
Yawning, stretching, groaning, and moaning
Going through our morning rituals
Our mind possibly in another place
The time of day quickly going, we must hurry

We jump into our vehicles heading down the road
The traffic delays us as we yawn and groan more
Not quite awake yet, "Oh well, just another day," we say
The anticipation of being late overtakes us
We start to panic and say, "Oh, just great!"

We cannot do anything about the ones in front of us
Our turn we must patiently wait for
We may groan and explode, "Get out of my way
I'm in a hurry," and possibly think
We are more important

We try to make them go faster
Those people who are in front of us
"Why can't you just get going?" we declare
"Faster, go faster for heaven's sake"
"I'm in so much of a rush now"
"Don't you people get it?"

It does no good to become all worked up
Everything will move in order and in its pace
We all need to realize we each have our place
Our space in the line in orderly fashion
We will all get to our destinations safely
That is what is most important

DARA MARIE

When we allow someone in front of us
As we try to give another a break
We pause and are thankful that others have done the same
We are all just as important as the next
Our turn will come again in time when needed

God treats us all the same, you know
His love never wanes for any of His children
What if He was in such a hurry?
If He pushed past to be at the head of the line not looking back
No time or patience to deal with problems or direct us

We are all indeed one of a kind
Each one having something special to offer
He does not care where He is in traffic
But we should all have Him
At the head of the line for us to embrace
The journey would be so much more orderly and calmer

As I have encountered my own heavy traveling time for years and after sitting in my own lines, day after day, this writing came to mind with, of course, a spiritual connotation to it. Yes, God is at the head of the line of life, truth, and love, but He does take the time for each of us with patience. Do we return it?

Grateful Heart

As the world seems to take possession of our being
Of our mortal situations, outcomes of circumstances
Let us all with grateful heart, with what we do have
Look upon the positives with quieted thoughts in reflection

It is easy for each of us, as I am included as well
On the mortal journey we all have to do
To think about what we do not have first
Let us all try to reverse the order of that

With grateful hearts for the many blessings we have
We can first be thankful for so many things
Cling to the positives, rather than what we may lack
Grateful thanks to the Divine would seem to be the first step

Putting out first the positive energy, rather than the negative
Then we can advance and be blessed even more
Declare our oneness with Him in humble gratitude
Then in total faith, we can allow the Divine to fully work

We each have to be diligent on this, as others even state
Reverse the negative power of thoughts and perceptions
Try to attain more of the spiritual in our mortal lives
It is waiting for us all, but we have to go and take the first step

I heard a story just the other day, televised it was
Of parents losing their child, it does not matter how
It would have been so easy to lash out with despair and hate
But they stated, at least they were blessed in having had him
Here on the mortal plane for even just a little while

They are more at peace now. Could I do the same?
Grasping, trying to understand the why
Never fully knowing answers to so many questions
But, in being grateful for having had their child at all
They certainly reversed any darkness of thoughts, emotions

They cling to the Light, which overcomes darkness
To the Supreme Creator of us all, they hold onto His presence
It is something for me to remember, as well, many times
Reversing negatives and keeping the everlasting light on
The greater peace attained, even in despair

We all have our mortal trials and tribulations
But each can attain so many triumphs
With grateful hearts, we cling and hold to Him
And in doing so, let more light shine upon us
As God touches us sweetly in our hearts, our souls

As each mortal day goes by, hour upon hour
I, myself, when presented things to overcome
Cling tightly to the one I know is always there
With grateful heart, above all else, I do try
I place my soul with Him and with a grateful heart

Harmony of Elements

A beautiful song is created and inspired
Each part of the melody carefully put in place
Inspiration from the Creator and the artist giving it life
And then the piece is given to the world

The union of both notes and rhythm
Combined with grace, beauty, and dignity
Sets apart one creation from the next
To captivate, to hold the listener spellbound

And so it goes and is accomplished by many
Two souls bring their own notes, rhythm into one creative work
Now called earthly marriage, the loving joining of two
Both bringing their own beautiful threads to the tapestry

As the journey of two continues on with mortal years
Remember during harder times why you were joined
As a beautiful pearl is conceived, some irritation required
Embrace the love, which brought you together

As each mortal day is presented to both of you
No matter how hectic the schedule seems to be
Treat the day as if the last you may have together
Always demonstrate the love and devotion to one another

Life is so short, here on the mortal plane of perception
The angry word or feeling may linger, even grow
All possible hurt must be resolved and quickly
Before slumber should be attained, for example

What remorse would there be
If the other never returned home to you?
Do not put yourselves in that position
The added hurt, guilt, anguish would certainly devour

Whatever may cause disruption, replace with resolution
Maintain that special feeling between the two of you
Such a treasured thing to protect and build upon
Let nothing put the precious union asunder

Hold firmly to the vows that were spoken
Remember your beautiful song, your tapestry, and the pearl
Love given and received by two souls embracing one another
Let the world take notice of your entwined love, the beauty

But, of course, it does take each doing this for manifestation

After listening to the beautiful works from so many wonderful musicians and then after my husband passed away, this writing was given life while looking back on our life together.

HEAL THYSELF AND RECLAIM YOUR TRUE PATH

When we have come upon a crooked path
We all need to be grateful for the ever-present grace
For possible wrong done to us being uncovered, revealed
For us to go on and in turn bless others, as we also receive
We then can be put back on our true path once again

We must, however, honestly look to what and/or who
May have put us in possible harm's way on this path
Perhaps someone whom we consider even a close friend
The culprit may be an evil influence of some other kind
In whatever form, mortal human or substance, it must be released

We all must come back to our truthful center again
Our inner core rediscovered and once more in place
Eyes opened, the evil influence now fully recognized
Yes, we have to do our part now in earnest
For the removal from our existence of the negative energy

Others that know of the cause and love us support and pray
They can continually work for our re-enforcement
The light from the Source, from our Creator
When our own heart is truly with Him, and we seek
The shower from that light down upon us, so very brilliant

If others have caused pain, sorrow for our heart and soul
With and from their influence upon us at the fork in the road
To make us stray from our true path, rightful direction
We can also pray they be healed as well, and it serves us to do so
The light can reveal many things for all and will; allowance

There is Divine love enough for everyone as the Creator gives
To receive and shine for them as well; their choice, however
Their heart can be healed; their awakening can be revealed
I pray that it will be for them, as well, released and healed
But reclaim your own true path with absolute resolve

Heal with Love

Love is the true, beautiful essence of life
The love of the Father to us and returned to Him
And the love from one to another
Behold the greatest gift we can give

Love comforts the downtrodden
Love heals all mortal wounds
Love transcends time and space
Love is all and remains true

As His love is given to and for all
From the everlasting and giving Divine realm
Let us all remain true in and with our presence
Love will heal, and the circle complete

Heal with love, and let love heal

Healing of the Delicate Heart

The heart is a delicate place
It matters not whether man or woman
When the chambers are filled with pain
It cries out all the same

We all have choices to make
Let the pain overwhelm and overtake us
Or ask that the pain be healed
To ease and cease, uplifting our being
For us to once again receive freedom

We all need to ask the questions
Why, who, what is involved
In our sometimes longing emotions
To have our heart feel love once again
From even a certain human being

We all want the same thing
To feel complete, to give and receive
We look in the wrong direction
The heart is again deceived

We withdraw into ourselves once more
To protect our heart from being hurt again
We must all learn from our mistakes
Realize not all are the same

Ask to be guided to your true someone
To the one who will gently love and cherish
To be ever-present for you in all things
Reflecting the beauty from above

It is our right to fulfill and be fulfilled
True love demonstrated for each
The peace, contentment, and blessings
To be not changed but enhanced
True love reflected in love
As our Father gives to us all

After encountering someone whom I was trying to make fit into my life from my own needs and yearnings and I thought was to be a romantic love, I quickly learned the lesson that some are not destined to fulfill that special chamber in our heart, nor should they. As we learn and work through these types of things of the heart, we also can keep the faith that it is better to have our true someone for us to fulfill, as well as be fulfilled by, in the area of romantic love. We must here again let go, let God guide us, and come back to center in and with complete trust that our Father knows best and will provide when the time is right for both to be blessed.

The Heart and Love's Reflection

In the quiet recesses of the heart
There is a very special part
Each chamber filled to overflowing
Where so many loving feelings roam

Love freely given to others
Love also being received
The hearts are both grateful
Love's reflection, indeed

Some people do not have
The capability, the understanding
When love is freely given
What can happen when it's achieved?

It is quite simple really
It amounts to just one thing
Love freely given to all
Love humanly received

Love, reflected in love

Holding His Hand

As I pause in peaceful presence
With God, my heart at rest
I am about to embark
A new and different life waits

I think as time has passed by
My daughter, my beautiful child
God's gift, my flower now grown
She now can smile, as she understands

All will be right with me
A new journey I am now going on
Not knowing for certain yet what will be
But God will be my guide

He will let me know what to do
Where I am to go
In peace and assurance, I am
He will take care of me
He always has

I pray to be His reflection
To express love to all
My task, my total understanding
Yet to be fully revealed

The new journey awaits me
Onward I will go
Clinging to His love for me
As a grateful daughter should

I am excited, waiting on my Father
The all-knowing, the great I Am
Praising His kingdom in my heart
Feeling and holding onto His hand

Even at my mortal age
Like a child I am once more
Looking up to Him for comfort
Feeling His tenderness, His love
I pray to my Father
Lead me in Your direction

I know I will be guided
I will try not to question
The new journey I take
Holding onto Your gentle hand with love

    This writing came about as I embarked on a new beginning, a new direction of fulfillment some years ago. We all can achieve our rightful manifestations when we each cling to the gentle hand of our Father as a humble child. May you each know a new beginning, a new direction, can always unfold for your life as well. Starting anew may take courage, commitment, but with Him, all things are possible. Follow your heart, your dreams, and be complete in peace as your new journey unfolds.

Human Shackles

There are those of us who have encountered
What seem to be self-created emotional shackles
Things that grab us and try to destroy
Our true being, thwart our rightful demonstrations

We all struggle with different human things
Coming into our lives, trying to overwhelm us
We each need to overcome our own situations
Never give in, keep going onward and upward
Obtain each success and gain our own birthright

The other side would so love to control us all
In whatever way, by any method it could
It is subtle at times and sneaky in its intrusion
In and through our thoughts, it would try to move us in the wrong direction

We all have our individual things to overcome
Let us not judge prematurely others' trials
We have our own human shackles to recognize
We all have our own seemingly rocky road to go on

But first recognizing these human shackles of our own
Clinging fervently to our resolve to overcome them
The key to unlocking the shackles is provided
We need to also go to the correct source

We then are all free to go onward with success
We should not criticize others for seeming weaknesses
Let us all remember we have our own work to do
The mortal journey of each in searching for our own answers

Let us then have tender thoughts for others
And put them with God's love, truth, and understanding
This in itself not only expands our grace
But also makes a declaration to overcome all evil

Many shackles would appear to hamper our growth
Not only for ourselves but mankind as well
Let us all declare Him, our Creator, the Supreme Force
And in doing so, the shackles for humanity
Will start being unlocked as well

This writing materialized when someone I was working with said, after discussing some very drastic things about her life, that she felt shackled and did not know what to do to come to terms with some serious issues. After searching for what those shackles were, she is now free, and life so much better. We each have to go on the journey of exploration in order to be free of even self-inflicted shackles preventing our further growth, expansion, and attainments. Use the Divine key to unlock your shackles and gain your freedom as well.

I Gently Touched Your Face

For just a brief moment, we were left alone
Words spoken, words being received by both
In soft gentleness, expression from each given
The feeling of no other presence except God

Feelings have been dormant for so long
Some never before really coming to the surface
You have touched me in such a way
Now I truly feel another gentle, loving presence

I thought I had experienced this before
As my journey through life went
But since I have encountered you
The best is being brought out in me

A softening I thought had been completed
Before God brought us together in His way
For a common mission for Him
And for the full realization of you

You are to take your special place
For mankind to embrace what you do and are
For you truly are in His service
I, but one human being, need to again thank you

You embrace gentle ways, as you are
He has surely molded and prepared
The best is yet to come for you
As you reflect Him, so it shall be

For all to witness how special you are
To keep giving of yourself as He has asked
Even though the road has sometimes been rough
The path is still clearly marked for you

You are to be all that you are meant to be
For Him, for you, for mankind
Know full well it will be accomplished
In spite of perhaps some human hurdles to encounter

When I said goodbye then
It was not to be a lasting thing
God's presence so strongly felt by both of us
As I touched your face with my hand and walked away

You remain with me still
Your gentle and sweet ways uplifting
Remembering the brief human moment
I looked deeply into your waiting eyes
And touched your face gently

Life presents us with many people who, if allowed to touch our soul, can receive what they need from us and can give to us as well. At times, we have no idea how their presence will bring dormant things to the surface for our own inner healing process.

This poem was written to and for a very dear friend. His soul presence continues to enrich me, even from a distance through his music that I listen to quite often. Do you have someone that has been in your life or the dream of someone in your future like this? It can happen with sweet resolve of thoughts and directions and, yes, putting your faith in our Heavenly Father.

I Have a Dream

I have a dream
It is called "The Bell of Unity"
For all mankind to ring out once daily
Three times

The pure tone can represent many things
The Father, Son, and Holy Spirit
Or perhaps past, present, and future
Each region deciding on its own

For all to hear
The tone so clear and true
To be placed wherever it can be
In each community, city
Large or small

To have each soul reminded
To pause briefly and reflect
To pray or meditate in his or her own way
The unity of mankind
To be reflected and uplifted

To be reminded once again
Of the Creator's love for us
No matter where we are
On our blue marble of human life

A tone so clear and pure
It will be heard above all
It will travel far distances
A reminder of peace, unity, and love

In reality, I know this is far-fetched, but many have had their own dreams come to fruition. If nothing else, my imagination took flight with the idea of someday, some way, mankind being united. It has to start somewhere, somehow.

I Pray for Music in Heaven

The emotion wells up inside of me, as I quietly listen
Beautiful notes and rhythms embracing one another
I close my eyes and absorb the melody being presented
How it feeds and nourishes my soul; I am so grateful

I find myself saying, "Oh God, thank You for those that create
The inspiration they embrace and I feel they get from You"
They go to the Source to receive their inspiration and share
In the process of their release; I feel so blessed in return

Not everyone partakes of what I call a feast for my soul
I feel such sadness for them in not feeling what I do
I feel and become more through the wondrous outpouring
I pray in earnest, though, for music in Heaven, at least for me

I hope and pray with all my heart, from me to You, Father
After human form is gone and I finally go to Thee
There is beautiful music in your Kingdom waiting
For me to love and embrace; oh, my soul will be so blessed

This is a tribute to all the musicians that have touched me in such a special way, as my own heart and soul have been allowed to feel so much beauty from their releases. Each one of us can be fed in this way, if we permit it. The rewards from listening and quietly pausing can be great and allow so much expansion for us as human beings. Find the music that feeds you in a positive way and soar with it to Heaven and beyond. It can be done and will nourish you emotionally like no other creative art form.

I Want to Dance with You All through My Life

Dance to the divine tones of life
Let the divine music flow to you
Embrace it and hold it tightly
Within your heart and soul

When troubled times come upon you
And being wrenched and seemingly pulled apart
Quiet your mind, go to God
And then dance with Him in soft reflection

There are many who also give us the music
That feeds our emotions and can even help heal
Find the ones that impact you the most
And bring forth their music to your senses

It is glorious to find both of these sources
For many are one and the same
So when you discover each of these
Dance through life with both eagerly

When times are wonderful, peaceful, and calm
Continue to dance through your life
Treasure the uplifting grace received
And I, for one, will continue to dance with you for life

If I Talk the Talk, I Must Walk the Walk

How easy it is to talk the Divine principles
To ourselves and pass on to others as well
There are many times, though, in our life
When we may find ourselves not doing what we should

A misguided thought or deed may transpire
Quietly and unobtrusively, it sneaks into our being
Human tendencies surface, and reaction erupts
Suddenly we are reminded of our own transgression

We all continue hopefully to learn in our mortal existence
To move forward and take our human steps to the Divine
When we realize what we may have done, not of God
We need to correct the action and be mindful of it next time

We regress and take one step backwards with humility
However, not deprived of forward Divine motion
But correcting whatever we may have done
So our footsteps can be planted more solidly on Divine soil

Fear not as we all continue on the Divine walk
Our salvation comes from admitting and learning from missed steps
This process is also part of elevation and healing
As we continue to grow and divinely expand

In talking to others, even if through the written word
I am also reminded of so many things
If I talk the talk, I must also walk the walk
On the Divine road towards my Supreme Father's throne

With humility, gratefulness, and love for His understanding
I will always try to become better for myself and for others
To remain always with Him and His never-ending light
I will continue to walk and talk radiating His glory, not mine

"If Only"—Unspoken Words, Deeds Undone

A very loving human being related to me so many times
Having remorse for not taking the time for another human being
Her schedule so very busy; we can all relate to that one
The unspoken words, deeds not accomplished so she feels

Now sadness fills her because the other has unexpectedly passed on
How many times, in my own reflecting on my past life
Have I done the same thing, but for whatever reason
The words or deeds were not brought forward, although the intention there

Since some of my own loved ones have left our earthly existence
The reminder now being presented to me of this from another
Has me sharing the sadness she is also feeling and the sense of remorse
How many times have I myself inwardly said, "If only . . ."

We all can feel the sadness, the pain but have to at least remember
While they were here, we did project love towards them in some way
I am now myself trying to be better at this during my human journey
Because I do not wish to say to myself once again

"If only . . ."

If We Run, We Cannot Hide

How many of us try to run from ourselves
To perhaps change the place we now live
New people, surroundings, we try to seek
Or try to escape wounds we carry deep inside

We think the changes are going to help heal
Somehow searching to escape the depths of despair
Or, perhaps, we just want to hide ourselves for the moment
Thinking the changes will make a temporary difference for us

Problems, hurt, the pain may subside for a little while
But there is still a time when it all comes back
We try to push it all aside time and again
However, it all still returns, the wounds deep within

I traveled overseas to a country and people I love
New customs, different basic living of gentleness
But still I carried with me some pain and suffering
They were deep within my heart and soul from long ago

I also need to deal with my own adjustments
Of perceptions, thinking, and elevated understanding
To try to heal the pain, suffering in my mortal home within
I cannot escape because where I go, they are carried with me

I will go back to where I came from, my birth country
Try to deal with what needs to be healed for me
When I go to a far distant shore again, in time
Let me remember I take my true home within me

It is better to return, familiar place and surroundings now
The customs known, as well as personally loved human beings
At least I will be more comfortable then, for the time being
And begin to take my problems head on, a must to perform

Escape to different surroundings, not the answer; it does not work
I take my heart, my soul with me, no matter what the mortal place
So I will return, taking home with me deep in my being
And I will continue to heal my home within first

This writing materialized when I was overseas in Greece and had a mission to perform. As I sat quietly in my hotel room, looking out over the beautiful sea thinking of so many things, this was presented to me, part of my own healing process. I have given this to a chosen few who were going through this very same thing, trying to escape, and I am grateful that it helped them also heal and understand that we carry a home within us, no matter where we may mortally roam.

The Illusion of the Mortal Reflection in the Mirror

We all go through human changes as mortal time goes by
The outside appearance continues to advance with human time
We can halt the progress for just so long, it would seem
Our inner core remains, the true essence, of course, the most treasured
     and important part

When we look into the mirror and notice the changes
The reflection is not the same, as human years advance
We all have our sadness because of the reflection seen
But we all must cherish the growth from within and continue on

The Creator blesses each one of us in His own way
Our capabilities, renewal, elevation, and expansion
We must all search to truly see deeply within our soul
We also need to look beyond the outside seeking another

There are many outwardly beautiful people here on Earth
We all encounter them on our journey in life
Many do not, however, possess the elevated perceptions
Thus, they are sadly lacking in so much for themselves

In looking in the mirror and seeing our human reflection
We all must realize who and what we truly are and possess
The reflection from our Creator is such a beautiful thing
When delving deep within us, we can then manifest Him

True beauty each one of us holds in radiant reflection
Is ours to embrace and expand on as we travel the mortal journey
Look beyond the mirror presentation and know
There is so much more that we can truly become deep within our souls

A beautiful reflection of our Creator

⌒∞⌒

This work was inspired from the musician Yanni's song "In the Mirror."

In Service to My Country

I am a soldier and serve my country with pride
Away from my human home and surroundings
From my loved ones and sense of security
In serving, though, I feel, I am protecting all I hold dear

As our national anthem says, "from sea to shining sea"
My country, my home so treasured by me
I put my life on the line for those I do not even know
As well as try to make humanity better, I pray

I endure much and have for centuries
Standing up for what I believe is right and true
I am proud to be in the service to my country
Side by side with others that serve as well

My family endures much along with me
They have to go on with their daily lives
They, too, miss much by my absence from them
But they also serve their country with pride

Even though I serve my God, my country in this way
How I wish peace would reign here on Earth
How extraordinary it would be for all to love
To have to care for one another just in our own land

Sadly that is not and has not been the way of it
However much I would love the reality as a person
To be less in demand would be wonderful
Peace for humanity, a most endearing thought

DARA MARIE

Then I could perhaps be with my own family
And they could be with me more and not be alone
But until then, I serve my country with love and pride
And try to bring peace to all, but I do take orders
I remain in service and take home with me in my heart while away

I pray for the madness to stop once and for all
For all mankind to love and embrace one another
To have tolerance, compassion, and give each other understanding
But, alas, sadly that does not seem the way of things
I cling still to the hope that one day I will work for other causes
In continued service to my country and others here at home

    This writing stemmed from talking to some service men and women I have encountered during my travels. This is a tribute to those who serve with dignity, pride, and hope, as they are human beings first and have their own dreams of fulfillment. Many have said the things to me that this writing represents, as they continue to serve and offer their lives for others. Let us not forget them and their families that also make many sacrifices along the way.

INFINITE POSSIBILITIES

Destroy the negativity of thoughts and actions
Think of what you wish to manifest
Then let go of mortal restraints, all of them
Think from the end, not the beginning

Triumph not a word but an action
Change your thoughts and change your life
If you want positive to happen, take positive action
And then rejoice and turn all over to God

Where your mind goes, you will follow
A change of mindset and feeling is a change of destiny
It is not how many times you may fail
It is how many times you get back up

Whatever you wish that is good and pure
Envision it already attained, mindset, you know
Then from and with mortal prowess
Continue on to and for the manifestation

Keep your passion alive and well within you
For the manifestation of all you may desire
It should already be in place deep within you
Now go, reach for the stars, and attain the infinite possibility

Into the Depths of Our Inner Being

When something in life jolts us to feel apprehension, hurt
Remorse, perhaps, or whatever deeply is affecting us
Whether it be the outcome of our own doing or not
We need to find the strength within us all
To be totally honest with ourselves and others

It is not always easy taking this task on
Finding the courage, digging deeply within us
To come to terms with an unfavorable reality
Perhaps it is something within us that brought it about
But it is always easier to blame others for the result

We all must be truthful with ourselves, though hard to do
Being content in searching and wanting the answers
We are not perfect human beings, any of us
But, we must all try and continually move forward
The well from which to draw the water of life's healing
Is so very deep, and there is an unending supply for each

In coming to terms with our human circumstances
No matter what they may individually be
We need to keep lowering our mental buckets
Delving into our depths with honesty, searching for clarity
And drawing the water, truth out from God

There are many currents that run deeply within us
Like the ebb and flow of the material earthly tides
Eventually it is all for one purpose, however
The constant movement so that the water does not stagnate
Life can be renewed, and the promise of fulfillment thrive

So it is with human beings, our deepest waters within us all
We must try to keep the water as clear as possible
With that, we allow our Creator to do this job with and for us
But we also must constantly allow our buckets be filled with truth
With humility lowering them into the Divine well provided
Into the waiting deep, still water of understanding

It takes work all of the time as our lives, like the tides, ebb and flow
The constant movement, the swirling between the still waters
Keeping our thoughts ever embracing our Creator
Trying to find the individual answers needed
And, at last, the sand is poured out, and clearer water provided

When we finally come to terms with ourselves, as well as others
Putting aside hurt and, yes, sometimes our own human pride
In honesty and then clarity, we then reach still waters
After going within our being into the deepest water
Of our astounding emotions, heart, and soul each one owns
Then this deep water of our inner core is allowed to heal

    This was inspired from the work of musician David Templeton, "The Deepest Water."

Joined with Love

Our two souls brought together with love
Each one holding the other in soft reflection
Our hearts, souls, and entire beings
Now united and announced to the world

"We are one now," the declaration has been made
Love softly and genuinely given, received
United now as one and blessed from above
The final vows to the world and Divine, now given

In harmony we now go onward with that love
With peace, joy, and hopefulness toward the future
So many blessings to receive by, and from this love
As we each give, each of us embraces the other

Both having gone on our separate journeys, so far
Now look beyond, the consecrated union now done
We are together at last, God's plan unfolded
We pledge ourselves to each other and to the Supreme

We promise many things to one another
In reverent vows of love and union complete
Let not the outside forces of the world
Erode our commitment to one another

Love reflected in love as the Divine propels
From above, it flows down to us, to all
Let us both now go forth in total embrace
And reflect to one another and to all others

The quiet voices spoken and whispered
From our Creator to us and beyond
Let us both make a difference to one another
And as we have said, "I do and will continually love thee"

⸎

This was written for a couple for their wedding ceremony.

Key to My Heart

There is a special place
I keep it locked
The key I have
To my heart

I want to release
What is now hidden from others
I am afraid, though
That the contents may be crushed

My heart yearns for freedom
To express what is felt
The dream of you
Oh gentle love

There are many chambers
To this heart of mine
Each one different
Filled they are to overflowing

The chamber walls feel strained
But "my someone" does not know me yet
So my heart remains locked
And hidden away for now

When my true someone comes
I will go and find my key
To finally unlock my heart
And share all of its chambers

The Key's Given to All

There are many ways and avenues we are presented with
The keys freely given to us all by others now and from the past
To open the doors of perception and understanding, to bless
To enable us to walk through them and behold the eternal Light

What waits for us on the other side of these doors?
Enlightenment, life, truth, and love radiating brightly
For all to embrace tenderly and become so much more
Then the mortal mind is awakened, and manifestations appear

We all need revelations depending upon where we are
Some are more advanced on the journey than we
But with the keys being presented to each one of us
We all must then recognize them, embrace, and react

The Source provides for all things and our right to have
We all have our own road to go on; the journey never stops
In recognizing and grasping gently but firmly the keys given
Oh, that is sometimes the greatest test for us all

Language of Love

I listened intently to the words from a man with God
Gently passing on words of wisdom to couples
"The language of love" he called it in his sermon
It did make an impression on me, and I will remember

He said there are five areas that bind hearts and souls
That couples should do for one another with love
Not once in a while but consistently
To keep the spark of love ignited for both on their journey

Each person in a union different in many respects
Some or each of the five components works differently
One or a combination may be more important than another
Take the time to find out, though, and watch the results

The five components he mentioned make sense to me
They are touch, talk, quality time, gifts, and servitude
Gifts not necessarily meaning mortal items
Or servitude meaning groveling of any kind

We, as human beings, also can remember
That our Creator gives us the same qualities
We all, however, need to do likewise back to Him
To the Father of us all and be blessed in the process

Touch God from your heart and soul, pure intent
Talk to Him often in thought or verbal commune
Quality time spent in quiet meditation to be nourished
Gifts to Him of obedience, faith, and reflection of Him
Servitude in trying to live our life by His commandments

We can all try to do the best we can to and for our Creator
Besides treating our loved ones like this as well
The flow back and forth when we all do this
The language of love is accomplished, how wonderful

Lessons of the Past, Promises for the Future

As mortal time continues on
And the recognition of lessons learned
When quietly going back to them in thought
Release the negative elements you feel
Rejoice in the lessons of the past

In taking the learning experiences onward with us
Understanding them full well, full measure
They also allow for our progression
The promises for the future, learned at the time
Will descend upon us as a soft and gentle rain

It also depends on your mortal attitude
Towards the lessons, manifestations, illumination absorbed
You can lament about the mortal strife in obtaining them
Or be thankful they indeed finally got through to us
Seek and find the promises of the future God has in store for you

Cast aside any false fear, disbelief that there are not blessings ahead
Listen quietly for the Divine voice given to you
Within each heart and soul; go quietly to His presence
True receiving has already taken place within
You then have to allow the lessons to penetrate

Cast aside self and go to the Supreme Father of us all
You will be directed to do many things, as you listen
Let the tones of the Divine bell that sweetly rings
Penetrate your entire being, your core
That is another promise He has given

While you may wait patiently, even beyond mortal limit
Know full well all will be given at the correct time
You are not to know the total plan
In faith, you must all continue to hold onto His loving hand
Another promise for your future He has given each one

Your mortal lessons continue as the journey does
But in taking each one with humbleness and gratitude
Within the sweet silence of peace and tranquility obtained
All will be made known as He unlocks the doors for you
Another lesson of faith in and with the Divine presence
The promise of and for the future

This writing was brought forth by something said to me in and with the sweet sharing between two human beings.

As we each may lament about the lessons learned, the trials and emotional torture, we can finally realize, if we allow, the lessons to embrace, teach for the future expansion of the human being. If we honestly embrace each one and then continue on with God at our side, the sweet tones from the Divine will be clearly heard. We all can rejoice, no matter where we presently are, in the promise of a better future, and armed with the Divine, we learn, grow, and continue on to the many possibilities that wait for each of us.

Letting Go of a Past Life

As each stage of mortal living passes
Whether in positive directions or not
Embrace the learning curves given
Abandon even the past aggressions

Forgive and love yourself enough
Know full well God, our Creator, understands
The different layers of mortal life
Contain many lessons in all of them

If remorse, guilt haunt you
As the new journey unfolds from events
Let go of the past baggage and gain freedom
Let them not hinder or weigh you unduly down

Relish in the goodness, even if the outcome saddens you
Or perhaps the loss of a loved one ripped at your heart
Either by love abandoned or not at all
Take refuge for your heart and soul

In order to heal and then continue on
Each mortal must come to the place
Letting go of a past life, mixed blessings, as well as strife
In order for the progression with God to continue

He has promised many things
To His children He loves
Put aside even past transgressions, pain
That, at some point, you do them no more

Love yourself enough, as His abiding love is yours
Not possessing a false ego, but stand up erect
Dwell in and with His presence; maintain the grateful heart
In order to receive His blessings upon you

Then whatever may be lacking in your life
With humble gratitude for His mercy and goodness
Claim it yours and then continue on
Embrace the good things of the past
Then your future can hold much promise

Let go of the hurt you inflicted or upon you
Whatever it is that pushes heavily against your heart
Let go of the past life, the negatives
In order to start refreshed, renewed and go on to . . .

A new and enriched life

This writing was inspired from two human beings in my life that are struggling with the same issue. As the writing was released through words, one has finally conquered putting part of her past behind her with finality, and the other is still in search of the reconciliations needed in order to overcome. I trust with time and patience, both will be blessed beyond measure, as they let go in order to obtain even more.

The Light, Reflection

When we walk into a dark room
We reach for the light switch
We activate it; now we feel safe
Ah light, we can see where to go

With our hearts, our minds and souls
We need to go to the Source
Illumination for us from God
Ah, the light, we can now see the true path

We will not be pointed in the wrong direction
Our footsteps will be sure, with the light
We will get to the place, our destination
Where we all need to travel on mortal paths

My thoughts also wander with love's direction
That mankind can do this as well
Turn on the light, the Divine, oh mankind
And walk with the Light, our Creator

Illumination from Him

Like a Child Once More

When we come into this world
Innocent and pure we are
We have not been exposed
To any evil influence

As time goes by, we learn, we grow
Eagerly wanting to now accomplish
All that we then have a developing passion for
All that we want to then experience

Then the outside world
Slowly and sometimes maliciously
Overtakes our minds
Overtakes our pure soul

We make human mistakes
We may suffer for them
But if we can remember
How innocent and pure we were
Who was in control of us then?

Our Creator Who gave us human life
Love eternal from His being to ours
We must go back to being a child again
To our Parent, ever-present God
And be mindful and obedient

Like an Abandoned Log

When your world is in turmoil
You seem to be an abandoned log
Drifting in the waters of despair
The waves, white with foam
Cresting and tossing over you endlessly
You may even feel yourself drowning

Pause and close your eyes
Be calm and reflect
Imagine a tranquil sea
Relinquish yourself to God
The calm waters will be
Peace and tranquility for thee

Release yourself and know
He will uplift your being
He will uplift your soul
The white foam subsides
Turbulence no more
We must know we are not an abandoned log

Bring yourself closer to the Creator
Ask and believe in your calm sea
You will be guided and protected
You are indeed a child of God
Feel no more like an abandoned log
Peace and love to thee

Like an Eagle Are We

The eagle soaring through the sky
Wings outstretched in full measure
Gliding on the airways of heaven
How beautiful an event

I watch in amazement, eyes focused in earnest
He gently turns and then glides once more
The magnificent display of air ballet
In pursuit of his prey, and he is committed

He carefully watches for movement beneath
His eyes ever scanning the ground
For it is prey he seeks
To swoop down on and be done

His talons outstretched in anticipation
For his prey is not yet found
He will be patient, though
Gliding on his airways of heaven

This reminds me that we are sometimes
Like an eagle; prey we also seek to grasp
God unfolding the understanding
Our needed nourishment supplied

We must also continue to glide
On the airways of heaven
Gently soaring, watchful, patient
Our quest not to be denied

When the prey is captured
The feeling of satisfaction overtakes
We partake and are nourished
Our goals reached—contentment, peace

We then soar again on heaven's airways
Gliding, wings outstretched
Swooping, watching for the next meal
To capture and partake

Eventually we are full on this journey
Our appetite somewhat calmed
Until the next time we are in need
Greater fulfillment pursued
We again glide upward and on

This writing materialized after I had been watching some beautiful eagles gliding gently on the airways around Anacortes, Washington, by the sea. They were hunting, and then gliding over the ocean, they returned to their treetop home on an island. They were so magnificent as they performed almost a ballet in the sky. I watched them for over an hour, as they captured me with their beauty and presence.

Little Log Cabin in the Woods

You are just a dream, a vision now
In my imagination, you have been placed
A little log cabin in the woods
A place of tranquility, peace, and rest

An escape for not only myself and my loved one
But also for anyone who wishes to partake
To smell the logs of which you are built
To relish in the stone fireplace and hearth

To quietly enter, no matter what the season
To absorb, renew oneness with God
Drift away with the needed thoughts
To heal, to re-nourish the heart and soul overlooking a meadow

Touch base with the Divine
In the little log cabin lovingly built
For anyone wishing moments or needing solitude
Or to embrace your special loved one

There will be a decorative wood sign
Over the outer door, carefully put in place
It will simply state this message
"Leave the Outside World Behind
Enter and Possess Love, Peace, Tranquility Within"

As one I love saw this vision before me
I now have embraced the possibility
There will be a little log cabin in the woods one day
To enter, give and receive what is needed

With pure intent, loving hands it will be assembled
For the purpose of love's divine presence
To bless others as we are blessed
I cannot wait for our little cabin in the woods one day
Lovingly united with the land God provided us

Little Rowboat with One

As I stand here looking out over the choppy sea
It is a little too turbulent, but suddenly you appeared
One tiny rowboat with just you in it, oh my
I personally think you are pushing it, crazy perhaps
But, apparently, you have the confidence to do it

As I sit here and write, watching your progress
Each oar in unison and making good headway
Even against the choppy water, you have faith
The destination you seek I feel you will attain
I still think you are somewhat in harm's way

Who knows or understands why you departed
Into the somewhat threatening open waters
From the safety of the shore, you ventured forth
It must be important enough for you to do it
To reach the distant shore is certainly your goal

As I am writing this down and watching you go on
Almost to the other shore you now have achieved
I am really amazed at how fast you progressed
Even though the sea seemingly would delay you
I just keep watching you and your absolute resolve

I asked the Creator to protect you from potential harm
"Take care of him," I said with my own resolve
Perhaps your loved ones wait on the distant shore
In faith on your ability to make the journey, you continue
Onward, ever onward, the little boat makes progress

You are now just a spec in the distance from where I am
What you accomplished reminded me once again
In faith and perseverance and the destination important
We all can make the journey we need to complete
Both oars going in unison and making headway

Each oar can represent many things or be symbols
But with each solid stroke, headway is surely made
Oh, if only we could all have the courage you showed
And the conviction as well; so many shores do wait
Each of us having our own little rowboat for one

    While living next to the ocean in Anacortes, Washington, viewing this little boat with one and during somewhat of a storm, I was transfixed with his progress to the other shore, which took over an hour of struggling. I thought his journey done, but after a bit, here he came again, back across in complete faith he would make it. He did, and this writing came into being from that experience of watching faith, progression even under some odds, and judgment, which I thought did not made good sense. It struck me that from this man having the faith and resounding purpose for the trip, all was accomplished, and he attained safe harbor once again. I pray each of you who read this will attain your safe harbor as well if and when needed.

Little Sailboat on a Tranquil Blue Sea

The beautiful blue sea so calm
Just enough of a breeze to fill the sails
Our little sailboat at first struggles
The sails are let out to receive the gentle wind

Slowly the sails are unfurled at last
To capture the gentle breeze given
Our little boat starts to smoothly glide
Over the blue and clear water
Destination not really important

Our little boat picks up speed at last
As the sails embrace the gentle breeze
The feeling of total freedom overwhelming
The cares of the world are left behind

As the journey of the day continues
Concerns from and of the world disappear
Left behind, they are in the small wake created
As our little sailboat continues to glide
Over and in the beautiful clear blue sea

How wonderful and calming the journey is
Sitting at the stern, nestled together
Arms gently around one another
The feeling of peace and love being experienced
As our little boat with us in it
Slowly making progress just for us

The open water at last reached
The horizon beckons to us to go onward
The possibilities endless, the journey so calming and true
In our little sailboat made just for two

When human time beckons us to return
The looks between us, the unspoken words
Oh, the disappointment, our freedom to end
The return journey, contemplation by each in silence
But we still peacefully hold onto one another

Each one embracing and treasuring the moments shared
The sails have to be lowered at last
As we continue on the journey back to the shore
The sense of losing being together peacefully and the freedom
In the little sailboat built just for two on the clear blue water

Although I have not experienced this as yet, while watching a beautiful little sailboat make its journey out to sea to the horizon with just two, my imagination took flight and thought how wonderful this might be. I will look forward to this becoming a reality someday. As my emotion also took flight, I could feel what it would be like in returning back to shore after such a beautiful day with freedom, love, and a tranquil blue sea.

Loneliness

One can be and feel so alone at times
In the deep recesses of mind and heart
It matters not whether in a crowd or by oneself
The wrenching feeling of loss can engulf

We can all go on feeling abandoned and having no direction or purpose
No matter when someone else tries to help
We all need to fill up our thoughts, our being
And be grateful for what we do have

We need finally to get humanly sick and tired
The overwhelming sense of isolation to be overcome
There was someone that told me long ago
"Pull yourself up by the bootstraps
Dust yourself off mentally, and go on"

We are all at times presented an unfriendly hand
On this forward march we all are on now
Reverse the negative thoughts and feelings
Put your feet back firmly on solid ground
March onward with confidence and love in your heart

Get over the sense of self-imposed prison from within
Our minds and hearts have so much room
In the simple acts of love and kindness to others
People will be drawn to us; retreat not, resume

We also need to go to others to assist when they cry
With support, we need to reach out our loving hand
There are many human beings to be discovered
With love and kindness in our heart, they will be found

And then when others have helped us overcome the loneliness
Spread the wonderful and joyful messages onward
They will do the same for others, rest assured
Before we know it, we are not alone in our minds and hearts
And we understand we never really were

And as the feelings of this loneliness depart from us
Actually we are never really singular, as we already know
God is always near and within each of us, standing by
And in doing so, the loneliness is no more from the giving

Love conquers all and radiates outwardly, our choice
And the blessings from it in turn continue to heal
Touching our heart and soul in unison, as we do for others
We are no longer alone; the loneliness conquered
The trick is in the remembering when it tries to engulf us again

This writing came about during a time when I was feeling very lost and alone. Even though I was surrounded by many people during the day, loneliness tried to engulf my being. When I finally had enough of the emotion, I went to God, and this writing materialized and helped me heal as well. May this writing do the same for all those experiencing the lonely times.

LONELY IN A CROWDED ROOM

I went with much delight to celebrate a family gathering
In Greece, new friends were found and asked me to join them
A place where food, music, and laughter were the norm
Around a large table, we all sat, adults and children

We talked, laughed, and giggled with carefree glee
Sharing stories, relishing in the wonderful new friendships
Then the three musicians came forward and played
Greek songs, music, and words filled the room, so beautiful

Lamented love expressed, dark eyes, and longing
I glanced across the room, quite handsome you were
Sitting with some friends, but I could tell
You were so lonely and lost inside yourself

I saw the pain on your face and could feel your aura
As the songs were played and words expressed
You glanced over to me, once in a while suffering
I wondered what you were thinking, such devastation

You exchanged words now and then to be polite
Your friends were pretty much keeping to themselves
You continued to just sip your drink of choice
Now and then glancing at me from across the room

I still wonder why or what made you so sad
You had a wedding ring on but no love at your side
Was there abandonment of dreams so hoped for?
You appeared to be lost, adrift on a sea of sad emotions

I know there are so many others that feel much pain
I too have mine every now and then, as life goes on
There can be so many causes; each of us has our own reasons
But the sadness—lost, empty, and adrift—appears the same

So much unhappiness and anguish for so many
I pray for each hurt soul to find peace, joy again
To find what he or she needs and so desperately longs for
It is devastating to feel so lost and alone in a crowded room

I have also been there, so understand

Lost and Empty Mortal Hours

My mind recalls lost and empty mortal hours
Times and moments that something could have been done
I am not talking about the needed human rest
But the periods when focused thoughts could have been
Projected outward and beyond to the Divine

Messages, directions to be sent and received
Healing moments in which much could be attained
For mankind, the world, for the universe
Embracing the Source, the positive loving energy flow

I could have made a difference in the past myself
Now I have been awakened more from mortal years
Unconditional love from above being the key
Now I try to extend more out towards whence it comes
For others with sincerity, and then it comes back to me

There is so much mankind can do, wherever people are
Treasuring productive moments for ourselves and others
Healing of hearts and souls, Mother Earth
In full recognition of Divine love encountered

Send the pure thoughts onward towards the galaxies
They will be returned in full measure as given
There is much to do and become for all of us
Each one has his or her birthright of attainments

Purification of our mortal thought, words, and deeds
Embracing quiet moments that we all should take
Letting them be productive for all good things, for us and others
With not so many of the mortal hours lost and empty ones
We each can make such a difference for ourselves and mankind

As the Divine reflection would say to all, "Well done, My children"

Lost in Your Eyes

Deep intense pools of brown they are
A most special quality within
As I gaze into them with mine of blue
My world lights up within me

I recall the first time we met
A smile to light up the world
You seemed to come alive as I did
And I felt your presence within me

Those pools of brown always remain with me
Even though apart, they are firmly placed in memory
As I close my eyes, I see and feel them
Those beautiful intense pools of brown

They are soft and gentle with depth
They show the true you to me
A sparkle every once in a while, though
As the little boy comes totally through

Then there is the serious, intense side
Passion held within and captivating my heart
They show the truth of you, even of pain
As we can automatically sense one another

Scorpio and Cancer we are
The recognition of many elements with ease
We can read one another quite easily
As we gaze into each other's eyes

The different emotions are experienced
Even though others may be all around
When I look into those eyes, your inner core
Oh, how they melt my heart

The understanding and love will never wane
Continues on with time, though now apart
You always will be in my heart with unconditional love
Your eyes will always be in my memory
Strong but soft, intense, passionate are they

When I gaze into them once more
The intense quiet touch of you felt throughout me
No words are spoken, and none are necessary
As I drift lost in the vast ocean of . . .

Your loving pools of brown

My hope is that each and every reader will have his or her own color of in-depth pools to draw from and unite with love and the deep softness held within each exchange. These kinds of moments are to be treasured, also recognized, as they are so very precious. As the sense of feeling lost in each other's eyes can send you beyond into the galaxies, I sincerely hope that each moment will be ingrained into you as if a bit of Heaven on Earth has been experienced.

The Love Chain for the World

A love chain is needed for the world
Each link strong and so important
Gently but firmly attached to another
Each one made from the same die, cast for strength

Each link of the chain having its own worth
Each tightly holding on to the next one
Firmly attached and making the chain stronger
Eventually to go around the world once

Then to the chain and the love it represents
With each link a human heart and soul
More links are added and then on and on
The love chain does in fact grow longer

In true demonstration and reflection of our Creator
Spreading the love to all people and lands
So it grows in strength and continues
Circling the world again and again

More and more links are added in human time
The fulfillment of each link attained
The chain does not tarnish from outside forces
Nor will it ever break but will remain strong

There are those who would try to cut the links
Weaken the love chain for the world in need
Obliterate the positive demonstrations from so many
But the links made from the same die lot
Never twist, never bend or separate from each other

And the chain continues to grow around the world

While seeing so many things take place in our world that technology has helped, seeing so much need, and seeing so many, many people rallying to and for the needs of so many others with love in their hearts, this writing came into being. Let us all continue to be a strong link for the world and not be corroded or weakened from the outside forces that would continually try to get us down. There is much more love shown than not, as we have seen during worldly disasters or in neighbors coming to the rescue of others, etc. In spite of what is transpiring from so much negativity bombarding our senses, the chain is growing stronger as mankind is becoming aware of many things and demonstrating more love to one another in so many ways.

Love from Above Casts a Long Shadow

Love from above, always present and upon us
Outstretched arms, making the sign of the cross
The Great Light shining brightly from behind
Casts a long shadow, touching all in heart and soul

It is always there, this great love, the shadow
I can see the effect on mankind over the ages
The long shadow embraces everyone, everywhere
To gently touch and caress each man and woman

The shadow cast is meant not to darken but to enlighten
We can step out of it and then into the bright light
The whole effect quite something really and ongoing
We, as mortals, have to absorb it all and pass it on

Then, we too, pass the shadow of love onward to others
As well as reflect and absorb the bright light
Of the night sky—the moon and stars—and the sun
One beautiful and purposeful radiating effect

Each one reflects and radiates from one Source
Mankind can do the same while here on the mortal plane
Each human being having his or her place in the whole scheme
Results in magnification of the great I Am

Love Is

Love is not cruel
Love is not selfish
Love is nurturing
Love is all giving

Love is tender
Love is sweet
Love is all
Love is seeing true beauty in another

Love is caring
Love is not overly critical
Love is forgiving
Love is compassion
Love is . . .

You fill in the rest
From the depths of your breast
That inner core of purity given
Love is all
Love is God

This poem was inspired from a Chippewa Native American who is coming to terms with his mortal issues and circumstances. In drawing from my own depths, the love that I try to possess, this writing was released. In and from the presentation, love surely extends beyond what is stated here. As we draw from our own deep inner core, what we extend to others we also have the right to receive. If it is not given from another, then we also need to let go and move on. Love is gentle, soft, sweet, kind, as God, our Creator, gives us His supreme love. Then as each mortal comes to terms with what we have and are in this mortal existence, we either have to step away to seek what we rightfully should possess in order to expand, be blessed, and feel the sweet reflection given back to us or remain stagnate, empty. As we are all vessels, let each one pour out the sand, whatever it may represent, in order to receive the clear water of blessings, renewal, and yes, love purely given back to us by our true someone.

Love One Another and Make a Better World

As we all proceed in going through our lives
So many things to accomplish, so many things to tend to
Other human beings depending upon us
We, at times, become overwhelmed by it all

Some situations harder than others to overcome
At times the demands on us overshadow
Our true reflection, our capability of just being
In peace and enjoying one another through love

It is so easy to be reckless with what we call love
To have it peacefully and joyously fill our being
Let it pour forth from within us to all
We need to pause each day
And take the time out for the quiet reflection

When we allow ourselves this time
To reflect and meditate with our Creator
We are then renewed and receive His ever-present love
Waiting for each of us to grasp, behold, and demonstrate

Then pass this love onward to all we encounter
Through a gentle smile, a word, a good deed, a touch
It is so simple really, and if more did this during their travels
Oh how much better our mortal material world would be
His love passed onward from Him to us, to all

Love That Lasts the Test of Time

There are some that experience this kind of love
No matter what trials or circumstances present
A love so tender, sweet, true, and dear
A love that grows and lasts the test of time

Two beings coming together as meant to be
Each bending gently and molding into the other's ways
In holding onto this incredible love that started
Keeping it tenderly and gently tucked away for them

Each breath so soft and gentle upon the other
Two souls embracing one another in understanding
In patience and tenderness, keeping it alive
Each being his or her own presence but united

This seems to be going away for so many
Each one has to elevate his or her thinking and pursue
Gratefulness of what is offered by the other
In order to keep the union firmly together

What a wonderful thing it can become
In softly saying to one another each day or night
"I loved you yesterday and love you today
And I will love you even more tomorrow"

The type of love that withstands the test of time

Love's Reflection

In the quiet stillness
Of our minds and hearts
We go to You
Nourishment to be gained
Peace to be obtained

Each human grasping
The answers to life being sought
So many questions
So many thoughts

We express our gratefulness
To You, our Creator
Life, truth, and love
We strive to be one
With Your loving essence

We need to reflect
To absorb and fulfill
Our destinies, our right
To be in Your reflection

To embrace goodness
Mercy and truth
Love to one another
As You freely give us

We must all bless others
As You embrace us
We go to You in reverence
Looking for our true essence
Love reflected in love

DARA MARIE

To give to others
In our everyday mortal lives
To be guided in all things
Love reflected in love

THE MATCH

The match is such a useful thing
A wonderful tool it is indeed
It just sits there, always ready
To light a fire, heat resumed

It is prepared to do the job
But it takes the human hand with determination
To strike something and ignite
The friction, the flame, fire the result

The correct ingredients and the right surface
Have been supplied for it to work
Now all it takes is the need to use it
Heat and ignition, warmth supplied

We have the right ingredients
For us as well, to be ignited and produce
All it takes is the right technique and having the passion
Then off we can go, as we too are ignited

MEMORIES

Sitting quietly by the sea and listening to gentle waves
Oh, the memories of times gone by come flooding in
Relishing them in the peace and beauty God provided
The mind escapes gently to the memories of life

Some of them are fleeting escapes to joyful times
In looking back, I also remember some that were harsh
But I choose to try to capture and hold dear
The ones that are and were so beautiful in blessings

The mind drifts like wisps of clouds against a blue sky
Floating from one to another in peaceful capture of form
Remembering people who have gone onward to Heaven
All of the treasured moments once shared with others

Once in a while, sad ones try to resurface and intrude
I do not want to go there, though, in thoughts of the past
I will cling tightly to the beautiful ones, if I can
To feed my heart and soul with the positives of life

I got through all the bad and sad times; here I am
I am so eternally grateful and feel blessed for so many
Because in emerging to the other side, as I have
I now look back and still came out on top from the lessons

Father of us all, I embrace You with love and gratefulness
I know and feel Your gentle touch and presence when I do
I remain in belief and faith in and for the future
There will be more joyful memories than not, my attitude

You will guide and protect me, this I know and pray
Your never-ending love, I remember well and feel
For it is You Who brought me out of darkness into the light
The constant reminder of the true memory of Your love

You are the ever-constant and loving Source to all
One of the greatest things we are taught along the way
The memory of that I clearly know and cling to
I pray the memories of my mortal life will be more beautiful than not

I, however, have my own job to do in constantly going to Thee

MESSAGES RECEIVED IN TIME ALONE

When we are quiet and still
In solitude with our thoughts
We consider ourselves alone
But are we really?

We can all go to the special place
That gently waits for us all
To communicate inwardly to our soul
We are never really alone

In the peaceful stillness of this place
If we concentrate and truly feel free
Messages are released gently to us
To receive and be oh-so blessed

If we remain true to them
Knowing and feeling them in our being
With faith renewed for the results
Messages are heeded and reacted upon

When we withdraw our minds
From turmoil and distractions
We can come to this special place
Our dreams and hearts to be fulfilled

The quiet place where love is given to all
Who truly believe they will receive
The heart and soul become
Once again content and released

So many things come from this place
Answers to questions
Creativity released for us to express
And we come to understand
We indeed are not alone

This poem was inspired from the musician David Templeton's CD *Time Alone.*

The Missing Link So Many Encounter

As I look into your eyes, a sensed certain look there
Yes, a sense of clarity, peacefulness is present
Something enters my own senses, however
There is still something missing; the eyes tell much
You are still searching, trying to define your missing link
Even though you would seemingly have it all now

You are looking out toward the vast horizon
Your eyes and mind seem intently focused
It is as if you, on your present journey
Are wondering, is there, should there be more?
There is something still missing in your life

There is a space in your inner core that feels incomplete
There are many others going through the same
Pondering the intense yearning, the dream
All you may feel, though, is a sense of being discontented
You may not even totally understand what it truly is

You search for this and that and even perhaps another
Trying to find the missing piece, you just sense a loss
You know in your heart and soul a gap exists
There is still a missing link, deeply buried within
So many others also encounter this same feeling

You may even think you are as complete now
As you are ever going to be, your destiny
But everyone needs that someone or something special
To fill the gap, to truly feel whole and fulfilled
To complete the strong qualities that you have

When the time is right for us all and we truly seek
When we are ready for the answer and in having complete faith
He, Father/Creator, will at last reveal and provide
The missing link, complete our chain, even to consciousness
That one thing we truly should have that He already knows

Then we will go onward with gratitude and proper alignment
In total bliss, the feeling at last of the heart and soul at peace
Each link of our being intertwined carefully now
The chain within us now stronger than before
The missing link that so many encounter, now, for us, a memory

This writing came into creation as I looked at a photograph of some-one, and in it, I deeply sensed something and recognized a familiar long-ing. I too have looked out to the horizon and have watched others do the same. The look, the presence, for all was there as well in the search for their missing link. From the almost sadness, the facial expression, the searching yearning eyes, and the body language, the feeling of loss was made known to the senses. If anyone has been to the same place, he or she can recognize that special understanding of heart and soul in others, a connection that many encounter. We are not alone.

Morning Java

Ah, the early morn did call to me
Even though I finally had a chance to stay in bed
But, alas, the thought of java did also call
So the covers were quickly flung aside
The feet hit the floor with earnest movement
To the kitchen they quickly did take me

Yawn, stretch, and the feeling prevailed
I did not really want to be up quite yet
But then I cast the thoughts aside
A day given to me by God for much
Full of opportunities, and I should be grateful

So I began to refocus from morn blues to rainbow
With a more positive outlook, I will embrace
There is no doubt I love my morning java
As I carefully measured the required dose
Something else quickly came into my mind

My thoughts turned to God and the love felt
From Him to me and then returned
Or was it the other way around?
As I paused quietly within, this came to mind
"Love beyond measure, as pure love, cannot be measured"
My java preparation now complete with the appropriate scoops

Every morning I will try to be more grateful
For unmeasured love from Him to me
I will return that love during my waking hours
And just before I lie down to slumber again
I will send my unmeasured love back to Him
No measured scoops will be used, as His love never is

My Beautiful Present

I received a beautiful package this day
The wrapping paper and bow of equal beauty for what it surrounds
I already know my package contains a treasure
The excitement builds in and with my anticipation

I carefully and gently begin to unwrap my package
The bow gently but firmly untied and then released
The paper lovingly loosened and gently set free as well
My anticipation builds as I take off the top of the box

I peel back the tissue paper that gently surrounds my treasure
I already know it is most beautiful, fragile, and I must take care of it
As I gaze at my treasured gift, I realize its beauty
I must take great care because it is priceless

I gently pull my treasure from the package
I look and study it with amazement and love
It will take me more time to fully appreciate its beauty
But I already know of the value of my treasure

It will always be the most beloved material gift I have received
Like no other I have ever had or experienced
It will take me forever to fully appreciate all the facets
But as I love and appreciate the entire gift, great care will be taken

I recognize, love, and understand all of what my treasure represents
As I study and relish each beautiful part that makes up the whole
It already has a special place in my heart and soul
It goes wherever I go and is with me always

Dara Marie

So I have carefully unwrapped my beautiful gift
From God, you were presented to me
I know full well and thank Him each day
And I have promised Him I will lovingly take care of you
My beautiful treasure, my beautiful gift presented to me

God comes first, and then there is indeed you
Where all love flows to and from
As children of the Most High, hand in hand, we go
To serve, protect, to radiate Him with love being the center, and for each
other

You, my beautiful treasure, I love beyond words spoken
You make my heart sing the beautiful music of Heaven itself
I float and glide with the Divine touch of Him
And having you with me makes the mortal journey so much more
beautiful

Love for and from Him, the Creator of us all
Love for you, tender dear heart of mine
The beautiful treasure and gift of both
Resounds in my heart and soul like no other

Forever

After celebrating the Christmas season, this writing came to me. Who
knows exactly what will trigger the creative content? Upon reflection, the
writing seemed most appropriate for human beings to reach beyond themselves and experience surrender of thoughts and emotions as I did in writing and giving birth to this creation.

My Chairs

A chair is such a useful thing
It stands and patiently waits
For someone to occupy it
Comfort given again

When it is filled
With human weight
It may want to sigh
It may groan
But it is giving support again

I often wonder
When looking at my chairs
Do they delight when occupied?
Comfort given again

Do they patiently just wait
For the human creatures
To occupy them once more?
Or do they simply sigh
And say, "Oh well, alone again"?

"I am here for you," they might say
"When you are all gathered
Treat me well
I will always be at the ready"

    While sitting with tablet in hand and looking toward my dining room chairs of comfort, this came to mind. Yes a lighthearted and rather silly something of subject matter, perhaps, but then as the imagination drifts, anything is possible within the human mind, even on the subject of chairs.

DARA MARIE

My Precious Violin

When I was but three, a violin I picked up and placed on my small lap
I carefully and tenderly put it onto my knees for supporting it
It was so very small, but so was I, at the time
Drawing the tiny bow carefully over the small strings

I must have felt it in my heart and soul that day
Even at a tender, young mortal age, the creative senses drew me
God blessed me somehow, letting me know even then
This was my instrument for so much joy and expression

My mother saw this take place during my time at school
The screeching sound to improve over time with lessons
The proper techniques to be learned to bear beauty of sound
The correct finger placements, the bow to be drawn with loving pressure

The beautiful music manifested with patience and practice
Became so much a part of me for so many years, a while ago now
Many years of joyful presence, fulfillment, and attainment
So many wonderful and beautiful memories I have now

I have not played for oh-so long, now it seems
I gave it up to be married and raise a daughter
But I never forgot the joy and my uplifted feelings
When playing my violin, the feeling of being with God

I will get another, better than I had before
I want to feel the beauty of my violin in my hands once more
Placed under my chin, in my arm, the bow gently gliding over strings
I will need to learn to read the notes again, however

To know what fingers go where, to make the music flow
But I know in my heart, soul, and from memories
When I begin again, it will sing to me once more
Oh, if I only had the mortal time to make it so

But, I will also cherish the memories of my creative release

✺

In this day and age, there are so many things that intrude upon our lives and affect the responsible decisions we must make, given the circumstances we are in. Many times, we have to make a decision on what is more important and what we devote our time to doing.

But in saying that, one can always return to the many blessings that happen from our sweet memories. Although I have the memories, as of this writing, I have not pursued my violin, but then I still have the opportunity to pick up my violin and play it again. I won't even be concerned about reading the music but will just let the notes become what they will become, as that creative process can truly bless one as well.

What have you, reader, left behind that you loved to do and release through your creativity? I hope you can also have the time to reignite a passion and soar with it.

My Special Rock of Three Hearts

While having my first visit to a faraway land, Greece
After a long journey settling in to a very special place to rest
I took a walk down to the sea, my renewal, water baby I am
There on a small, secluded beach on the Gulf of Messinia, I did pause

The water so clear, the beach with small rocks, pebbles, and shells
Sitting there by water's edge, the mind and heart drifted to heaven's gate
My thoughts projecting especially toward one and the family
With love, gratitude, and never-ending faith, the mission

I meditated there for quite some time, casting thoughts to the horizon
I asked to receive something very special to take home with me
My visit and commune to be remembered and marked
I asked God, "Let me find what You want me to have, a sign"

I started glancing around and then got up to walk the beach
Asking to be directed to find what I was to have, His choice
A gray nondescript rock called out to me, the energy from it
"Pick me, turn me over; I have a hidden treasure for you"

I gently complied and picked you up, turning you over in my hand
As I glanced down, three distinct heart shapes intertwined
White ribbons of deposits from long ago making the design
I smiled, said, "Thank You," and gently put you in my pocket

I knew I had to take you home with me; I treasured you so
I humbly had asked and received a most precious gift
You could not have been put back to join the many others
You were clearly meant for me, my rock of three hearts from ages gone by

I have shown my special rock to some chosen others
Being curious on my part to see if they could spot the design
Of all the ones I have shown this to, only two others could clearly see
One my daughter, the other a loved sister now

All three hearts are gently connected to one another
From ancient times gone by, you have been where?
My very special rock that called to me among so many others
I am so glad I picked you up and tucked you away

In a closed cabinet, you are now placed and secured
Every once in a while, I pick you up, feel your energy, and smile
Remembering the special moment I was directed and found you
A special nondescript rock on one side, but you were meant to be mine

I was supposed to have you, a sign of the past, present, future perhaps
I am not sure of your exact meaning to me, but it surely represents love
In time, and further understanding, I will possibly know more
Why I found you, a rock representing love, just for me in Greece

I have returned to the same beach, different trip and time
I have found another rock as I asked; it also called to me
This one a different message, but I used the same technique
It is now lovingly placed beside my rock of three hearts

Both are now blessing me with signs and memories

Nadir, the Lowest Point Reached

In our lives, we all have experienced more than once
Depths of despair and the feeling of being overwhelmed
We, then at some point in this human life of ours
Reach upward, pleading for help, for our answers
For the calm, still clear waters to materialize

When we are happy and content, our lives in balance
We feel we do not need the release, looking toward the Divine
But as all feel once in a while, things seem to crash
Our lives, our hearts and souls become so burdened
The sadness and despair seems too much and overcomes

During these times of despair, the lowest point reached
So many of us immediately reach beyond ourselves
We reach towards the higher power we believe in
Heaven's gate, the doors open, the angels speak
We must listen, however, the real test for each

In faith, sometimes tears being shed, we release
Asking for Your help, Father, our direction to seek and know
We then can receive the love being showered down
And, at times, the answers themselves surprise us
We may even try to dismiss them, flooding our mind

We at times fight them; "Not this, it cannot be," we may say
But then, at our lowest point, when finally it is reached
The growth of us always the test presented for each one
We finally, in quiet calmness, listen and then agree
And we then can go onward, the quest for the ultimate
We can all call them our loving demonstrations from above

This poem was inspired from musician David Templeton in his
CD, *The Crossing*, and the creative work "Nadir" in his CD *Change*.

Never the Same

There are so many different paths one can take
On life's journey from childhood and beyond
Each experience presented, whether good or bad
We are forever changed in some way
Depending upon how we deal with each one

With renewal, resolve, acceptance, or denial
Each triumph, or even supposed defeat, changes perspectives
We can rise or fall, depending upon our own choices
To be chained or obtain freedom and on to expansion
Through mortal or spiritual perceptions, the choice

The simple lessons learned while being young
Can alter so many things, as each individual advances
Going forward or backwards, here again mortal choice
But we all are never the same from our experiences
It is how we view them, here again, mortality

How I wish so many things were clearer to me
But, I suppose, the journey for each
At times almost feels like two steps forward
And one step backward; "This is tough stuff, being mortal"
Then I must either pick myself back up or just stay put, stagnation

My mind drifts as I try to imagine, during my quiet pauses
What waits on the other side of mortal life, when release given
I can determine, however, how I will be now, this time
In and of this mortal containment, in human form
We all will never be the same after the transition

To beyond . . .

No Distance Too Great for Love

Even though we may be apart
You are forever and still in my heart
Remembering the sweet embraces
Full of love being given and received

To know the other feels the same way
No others will we have or need; our fidelity
Until we are together once more
Our love for each other remains

To anticipate being together again
Looking into the eyes of the other
Just knowing you are mine
I am yours, you must know

Forever in and through pure love

For this poem, I received inspiration from the CD *Promise* by musician David Templeton.

NOBLE NATIVE WARRIORS

A noble native warrior has now ascended
To your ancestors, you are now joined
The great past spirits from long ago
Open their souls to you with soft embrace

They lived with honor and mortally passed away
Their heritage left behind, now yours as well
Still so noble, as you are all joined together
Now you have become a past spirit yourself

The strong legacy you left in your wake
Homage to Mother Earth and all her beauty
The creatures that roam upon her
You honored and gave thanks for them
A simple hard life you had in bygone days

In this present time, your people are still struggling
The elders try to pass on the traditions to the young ones
To keep the past ways and the heritage values alive
That you so lovingly wanted to leave behind

Another warrior has now joined you
He may have walked the double line
Of present times, but his heart and soul, native
You take him into Heaven now to be with you

Oh, noble warriors of the past
I extend my honor and gratitude to you
Even though I am not of native heritage
I send you my love for what you instilled for and in mankind

You roamed free and honored the land, what was given
All animals, trees, water, life, all elements
You continually touched base with the Great Mystery
Even though mortal life harsh, you still survived

Now I write this creative work
As one warrior has departed back to you at Heaven's gate
Upon his trusty steed, with head held high, triumphant
He rides steadily onward and upward to join you all

I know you will take good care of him
Another and different realm you all abide in now
But, rest assured, your presence here
Is still strongly felt and extends beyond

The children now try to resolve
What the proud heritage means that you left behind
Modern times, elements push against their hearts and souls
I pray there are enough true souls left to teach them

True ways of living with gratitude
Honor and respect for what the Great Mystery gave
As I cherish a noble warrior now and always will
I again say . . .

Thank you for leaving your legacy and ways behind for all

　　As the creative work came to me quite unexpectedly one evening and really not knowing specifically who the ascended warrior might be, I decided to offer this in honor of those native souls who still try to exist with their true ways in this modern age. The noble legacy left behind from their past spirits still lingers through time and space and provides a true magnification of what they once were. This legacy others can now embrace and continue to try to hold as people, a noble race, put upon this mortal existence by the Great Mystery so many call God.

THE OFFERINGS

The sunrise bursting forth
Beautiful colors exploding
Quintessence of light
Liberally showering the sky

The promise of a glorious day
The warming of the heart
The blush of the light
Illuminating the darkness

Upon reflection of this event
We all can feel God's love to us
A reminder of Him to be absorbed
The heart surrendering once again

When the sun withdraws slowly
Gliding to the horizon
Displaying beautiful colors once more
The end of a wondrous day

The regret with a saddened heart
The departure—impending darkness
But with the understanding and calmness
The offerings will continue on

The recurring cycle
Every new day beautiful as the one before
In appreciation of the gift presented
Mankind should pause in anticipation

Be still and at peace, wait to be blessed
Watchful in wonderment
The gift freely given of love
God transforms our understanding, illumination

Pause and watch when you can
Take the time in quiet abandonment
Not in every day this can be seen
So relish in it when the offerings are presented

Having experienced this quite often, I and others feel truly blessed having this most precious gift. As each part of the world goes through the normal cycle, we can be grateful for the morning and then the ending of daylight. With a cycle completed, we can look forward to each possible offering, no matter where we are located on our blue marble.

Oh My Child

I helped give you mortal life
And now you have departed this existence
Your journey here so brief
As you have now gone onward to Heaven's gate

Although we may seemingly be separated
Not so, I cry out in my heart and from my soul
Because of love, we are still together
You just have gone home before I have

You, my child, are now at peace
You have left behind mortal plane
The Father of us all now has you in His realm
Life eternal now lovingly caresses you

The bond of love, always so strong
Our hearts and souls connected as one
I may grieve at losing you here
But with faith and belief, you are now free

Free from mortal trials, pain, anguish, and despair
Free to flourish, continue to grow and blossom
Free to be the beautiful flower in Heaven's garden
Free of mortal bondage as the release has happened

The mortal years will pass for me
Remembering you and your true essence
That will keep us together, love, you know
Never-ending love as our Supreme Father has for us

I will see you and feel you
This I know from our bond
Love transcends time and space
It never ceases between us

As a warm soft summer breeze
Brings about a sense of sweetness and comfort
Catch the moonbeam or the sun's radiant light with a kiss
I fling them out toward Heaven's gate to you

I close my eyes and see you
With a radiant, peaceful smile
Joy's abundance surrounds you now
Because you are free and with our Supreme Father

Other family and friends that remain here still
Will experience the heartache from your loss among us
But with time, prayer, and comfort from others
We shall be united, calmed with and from the Grace of God

Oh my dear child
You were first God's, then mine, and ours
We send you our love from here to there
Remembering, embracing you

Serene angel, you are now

    This writing was done for a memorial service for a young woman who had unexpectedly passed away. I wrote it for the mother, and it was read at the service. The content of this writing can be for anyone lost, whether child, spouse, brother, sister, father, mother.

OLD BAGGAGE

When you finally encounter
Your companion in love
You may have baggage
Another life left behind

But when you gaze
Into each other's eyes
Your heart tells you
This love is so right

To love and be loved
In sweet and resounding bliss
Let go of the former baggage
And start anew and refreshed

A new life, a new beginning
The combined journey to anticipate
Each one giving and sharing
How beautiful, a renewal for each

So much love and joy
To give and receive
A new beginning for each one
Open together your door of life
Leave the old baggage behind

The Old Tree

A giant tree stands in the meadow
Its large trunk erect and straight
Taking on the weight of its branches
It has its own presence—mighty

It is so perfect and beautiful
I sit down under it and look up
As my mind wanders to another level
While I quietly contemplate in serenity
It reminds me of something else

Our Creator is the massive trunk
The large older branches are past generations
From them smaller ones branch out
Extending outward from them, reaching

From those smaller ones are generated
All reaching for the light, the sun
Each one unique, having its own form
Smaller ones again extending from them

On and on growing, ever flourishing
The leaves, beauty of adornment in their season
Bursting forth on command with the cycle
Oh, what a beautiful thing it represents
This old tree standing in the meadow

How alike we all are, heritage of human beings
The many branches of the tree, the new growth
Continually nourished and supported
By the massive, old, but sturdy trunk

Our Creator

Once a Home

I have a dwelling where I live
Considered my home a while ago
Comfortable and cozy it still is
So many memories—the mind roams

Then the loss of my loved one
The same feelings slowly fade away
Now it is just a house to me
I no longer feel it is a true home

It is just mortar, brick, and stone
Walls upright, plenty of space
Yes, a comfortable house
But it no longer holds me to it

I look around my house
I realize what it now has become
What made it feel like a home?
Empty spaces now exist

This dwelling I reside in
A house, not my home any longer
When your loved one is gone
Then you realize at last the difference

I will leave this place now
Taking some wonderful memories with me
My mind, heart, and soul are my home
Comforted by God, no matter where I roam

Perhaps God will grant me another
Companionship and love once more
We will find another dwelling
And it will become another true home just for us

Dara Marie

As of this writing, I have another home surrounded by the tall evergreen trees of a forested landscape, plus the mountains, ocean, lakes, and streams of the Pacific Northwest. I fell in love with this beautiful area, and it services me with peace, quiet, and beauty. I do have a home. Although not yet complete, the heart and soul are quieted for what needs to be accomplished at this time.

A home is where the heart, or comfort level, is. Or we can call a place home for a time, depending on what is going on in our mortal life. Here again, we need to allow the pause and trust that God will provide us with His blessings when it is time once again to move on, if that is what we choose to do.

As I put out the finite request to the real estate person, my entire wish list was brought to fruition, so once again, projection from thoughts, words, and Divine action become reality.

If you are not comfortable in your home, whether single or not, take the joy you have and project what you wish for. With perseverance, you can find your next material home if that is what is needed. But always take your home within with you.

Our Answers for Life

Oh life divine on Earth
How we grasp at you eagerly
The promise of fulfillment
To have and to hold tenderly

As our journey continues
Through this mortal life, existence
The realization that we know so little
So much for us to learn
So much to be gained

We scrutinize each human step
Reaching for the answers
Life to be presented
Needing our lives to be enriched

At times, we groan, we moan
Our human footsteps unsure
Paths sometimes full of twists and turns
Which way is the right direction?

We cry out in anger at times
Not understanding how or why
But we all must go to the place
Knowing You, Father, our guide

The understanding finally contemplated
Our inner strength renewed once more
We can then go on with true direction
From You evermore

Our Blue Marble

Man cries out, "Where are you, Creator?
Why have you forsaken us?"
The world in so much turmoil
The world in so much pain

Mankind must come to know
You are ever-present at our side
You are life, truth, and love
Eternally given to all of us

We state we are Your reflection
But we often go in a different direction
How then can the realm of mankind
Reflect Your kingdom?

You ask much of us, Your children
But You have given so much in return
Our beautiful blue marble
In which to have our human existence

We wonder why there are
Such horrendous events occurring
Human beings attacking one another
The weather in turmoil
Our Mother Earth rumbling

We ask, has our Creator abandoned us?
Where is He? We need protection
We must all ask ourselves
Are we being His reflection?
We need to go down on our knees
And ask His forgiveness

Our blue marble continues to turn
In perfect unison with the rhythm of the universe
As He has ordained and planned
The forces keep our world in its place

We are abusing our blue marble
Our Creator has lovingly given to us
Destroying, absorbing, ignoring
Her beauty will not last

Mankind refers to our marble as Mother Earth
But what are we allowing to happen?
A mother's love given, nurturing us as we grow, exists
Providing all things to us we humanly need

He has commanded we honor our father, our mother
Humanly speaking of course
But does this not apply also to Him
And to our Mother Earth?

Wake up, mankind, and plunder no more
Realize where we are all going
Where we all may end up
Our little marble decaying, our Mother Earth destroyed

And then what?

Our First Meeting

Reality

We met quite by accident
Or was it? I don't think so
As I gently smile in remembering
Oh, that first encounter so beautiful

You looked up as I approached
Your beautiful smile radiating so much
Mine as well, as you walked to me
The heart and souls of each one touched
We both felt God's presence

When you thought I was leaving
After small exchanges of mortal words
You came over to me and gently said
"I have to tell you something"

"You are so very beautiful
I had to say that to you
I do not say this to just anyone"
A soft smile on your face, your eyes tender and true
I felt the souls connect, and so did you

Others might scoff at this seeming ploy
It was no game you were playing
Those moments spent with you
That first meeting, just for two
Happens when truly meant to be

We parted that day, no phone numbers exchanged
There were no further inquiries made by either one
Your heart spoke, "I will be back and see you again
We will be placed in each other's arms one day"

I am not an unrealistic dreamer
I keep my feet firmly planted on the ground
You knocked my socks off, though
I am still in search of them, as I told you

Lightning bolts and volcanic sparks through the air
Felt by each one, but oh, the softness expressed and received
I will never forget our first meeting
It was surely meant to be

You have told another, "Her soul called to me"
I have said the same thing about you
It goes well beyond the appearance of the outside
Hearts and souls were combined instantly

I wonder how many others ever encounter
This beautiful and radiant first event
You have touched me like no other
The immediate recognition of something
Beautiful, astounding, and harmonious

Since this was all witnessed by two
Whom I dearly love and treasure in my life
They saw the connection, sparks, the volcano blasts
Reaching to the stars and well beyond by each

As the journey now continues on
True love being expressed and deeply felt
How amazing it all is through even time and space
It happens for one another when true and pure

Others do not even have to understand it
Some will dismiss it as being a dream
If they do not have the comprehension, let it go
We know what is happening and why

It starts from above in having faith; it is so
Being guided and directed from His Love
Now being expressed, as meant to be
One to another, as hearts and souls are connected

You have touched me in so many ways
I know the first kiss and true embrace
Will confirm how we truly feel
The sweet essence and beauty of it all

There is so much more waiting for each
The blending of two and in support of one another
To continue on in our human and spiritual life
As we fly to Heaven and back
From each kiss, each expression of love

How beautiful and wonderful it is
To have these feelings already within us
When the time is right, oh, the blessed journey
Clinging to one another with hearts and souls intertwined
Even more treasured moments to experience

I know why, how we were brought together
We were joined in unison before
We know and feel so much already
Through spoken and even silent words

I will love you as much or more than I did before
You will protect me, and I will protect you
I do and will love you like no other
You, in turn, will also do the same for me

The Dream . . . Beyond Reality

As I gently place my loving arms around your neck
You embrace me to your being and hold me tight
Gentle smiles, eyes in soft surrender to each other
Heaven's gates pour forth the pure love

We may question, why have we met at last?
We both had our own journeys to go on
But God has gently pushed us together
As if He said, "My loving children, it is now the time"

We will feel complete and bring out the beauty of the other
As we cling tightly to love, thoughts, and being
We leave the world outside, and dwell on our own perceptions
We are one and all that matters in these moments

As we look into each other's eyes
The heart pounding because of how we truly feel
Soft smiles of complete understanding given to one another
We thank God for our blessing of true love

There is nothing to mortally compare to what is felt
The hearts and souls truly connected, and beauty reigns
You make me feel so beautiful from within
I know I do the same for you

As God smiles down gently upon us
We recognize the true reflection of Him in our lives
As we embrace one another, His beauty and grace felt
We are so grateful that at last
We have found one another as meant to be now

I gently place a soft kiss on your cheek
You hold me tightly to you with your strong arms
There is no other feeling like this
Heaven is surely felt from just this alone

As the beautiful music softly plays in the background
Holding each other in soft embrace
No words need to be spoken, the ultimate presence
Heaven's gates open, ultimate love felt and drawn upon

Even though mortal distance may keep us apart
We are still with one another, tightly holding on
True and lasting love given and received
The soft touch of God's love felt by both

As our journey continues on with one another
Moments of flying to Heaven and back
The soft and loving touch and words expressed
We are so thankful for each other

Clinging to one another on a beach, listening to the ocean
Staring up to the clear sky, looking to the stars
That special feeling of these moments
Remain with us always, as we both simply say

"Thank You, Creator, for all; we are now both complete"

There was an encounter like this, but "beyond" above never happened and reflects the dream many of us create in such situations. We are presented people at times thinking they are something they truly may not be. Be wary and do not be the one who may react too quickly and not allow enough time to get to really know the other person.

The meeting did happen, and I thought perhaps things would work out, but alas, this person entering my life had another purpose, his own agenda, and the lessons taught, although difficult to accept, are now worth more than the value of gold. He ended up being what they call a parasite, and yet I finally recovered and have gone on even stronger than before.

We need to embrace the lessons we all receive, let go of the heartache, and forgive others as God knows all. They will have to deal with the outcome from their own actions as their life continues. In giving our forgiveness, because they know no better or don't care who they use, we receive our own freedom. Do not let a dark-energy influence take over your own being. In the forgiveness, there is the freedom we obtain, and we remain fully aligned with God.

Our Ink Cartridge

A pen is a very useful thing
It glides and flows on the parchment
The words expressing what we feel
What we need to say from us

Without the ink, however
No thought, no words expressed
There would be no communication
It would be a blank parchment

We are like the pen in some ways
We all need to have our ink
To be able to express what we feel
To be able to communicate

We all need to have our cartridge full
Instead of ink, a beautiful soul
In order to do this
We must be full of God, of love

After writing and my pen ran out of ink, my mind wandered and started thinking about human beings having their own spiritual ink cartridge, and thus the writing developed.

Our Strength Renewed

As things occur and are presented in our lives
Different events, situations to each one
We are humanly thrown at times
Our emotions become raw
Our resolve is threatened

We may feel lost, confused, and empty inside
We may not know how to handle our thoughts and emotions
The light of our inner core diminished
It feels as if it has been minimized

Know full well from where our strength comes
He is ever-present to rekindle the light
Our inner core, our strength ablaze once more
Declare this for yourself and for others

We should not let the human disturbances of life
Deter us from attaining our true being
Our birthright to have and behold
Know full well His light shines brightly

We have but to declare this for ourselves
We are His reflection, and thus we are healed
Our strength, our true being, our inner core
Once again is renewed and becomes stronger

    I have traveled this road more times than I can count, but each time
that my resolve, my inner core is threatened, I come back to center once
again and find renewed strength to tackle what I must.

Our Wick, Our Flame

The flame on the candle
Magnifying a beautiful glow
How it darts to and fro
Depending on the air flow

Sometimes it seems to stay still
Other times it gleefully dances
Swaying from side to side
But its light ever constant

As I sit and watch the flame
I quietly reflect and meditate
We are like, in many ways, the flame
Striving constantly to maintain

Life encounters, like the air flows
Sometimes peaceful, other times troubled
But if we maintain a strong center core
The flame may waver but never wane

It will stay constantly illuminated

The Pain of a Child

When someone, especially a human child of ours
Goes through so much on his or her journey
We can see the pain and hurt, the despair
In the face and in the voice being expressed
"Oh, I want so to help," we say

We ourselves have been on the same road
Twists and turns so unkind at times, many the same
We remember them so well now
We want to make it all better and resolved right now
Just snap our fingers, and everything will be healed

We recall so well our own anguish and pain
Tears flowed from us as well during our times
How did we ever get through it all?
Ah, but then when we quietly listen from within
We remember all was a lesson to draw from

Even though the hurt may be rekindled for us
In thoughts being brought to the surface once more
By our own human child now experiencing what he or she is
We must put our human child back with God
Our Source first, steadfast and foremost

We can try to help the other cope now
Help the pain in the heart subside and heal
To attain a higher level
To reach up with heart and mind
Draw from the full and pure well, God

So many lessons, so much hurt at times
Our heart being one with the other, our child
We are in anguish as well because of the connection
We may realize already the answers for the one
But each must get them, and each one different

The tears being shed for our child during this time
"Oh, child of mine, do not hurt," so we say
I imagine the Creator says the same thing to us
But so many times, we do not listen, even still
And we have been on our own bumpy roads
Even, at times, the same ones presented

And so, we, as well as our human child, continue the journey of life
Going through the times we do and on the wrong path
From our human will or lack of understanding at the time
We all can come to the place of shouting and screaming out
"Oh, help please, Father/Creator of us all"

We, as human parents, think our children are now recovered
The latest hurdle, the last one for them, we pray
But our human existence always has challenges
One thing for certain, our love for them never ends
Like our Father in Heaven, ever-present love

We are all His children, and He is always here to guide
We try to tell our own children this so many times
Continue to pass on the love and understanding
But they still have to get it for themselves
Then the lesson to be learned is truly theirs

As a parent myself, when my daughter comes to me for help, support, love, understanding, I pass on my own learned lessons the best I can. Many times, I think she does not get at the time something I lovingly remark to her, but it comes back later as she recalls what was said. As a light bulb is turned on, she then gets it and continues to receive her healing, enlightenment. Only when each of us is in that certain place can we then receive our own revelations in our own time.

Past Dreams Remembered

Some years ago, I started having the same dream
The same one repeated itself over and over
I thought I just liked the storyline
It was quite intriguing, really something

I thought I was making it up in my subconscious
A self-perpetuated dream of fulfillment and love
We were back in time, oh peaceful land and people
Mother Earth and all living creatures were treasured

Now that I have gained some further perception
And after now meeting in this time of our lives, once again
You are exactly how I remembered you, even outward appearance
Long, oh-so long ago in another life, existence

When we met this time around, the plan from the galaxies
Our souls immediately connected with the same energy
We even now communicate to one another when apart
Time and space, mortality of no consequence

I never really thought about this kind of thing much
Besides, I did not have the understanding then of this
Each soul lovingly feels the past connection
We each have had the same dreams, now shared in detail

How amazing it all is, looking back to years ago now
In remembering the dreams of the past, so wonderful
As our past love was combined together
I pray next time I will again remember this love

But this time around, it is not meant to be, and I leave that to God

I have talked with many people, as they also have had this happen to them, and it is not unusual as I once thought it might be. When we allow the mind with and to the Divine connection, we can be very surprised. We all receive what we are to receive, and then when reality comes about, why are we surprised, even thrown at times? Here again, keeping our spiritual faith in place, we all must keep our feet on the ground as well, with and in reality.

This person, this time, did not match up to the past experience, so I assume it was not meant to be. But some such meetings are indeed united from and with soul connections in the full expectation of what happened in the past.

When something like this happens, it does not even have to be a romantic union. I know a woman who now has a soul connection to someone who feels like her brother, yet she has never met him. And so it can be.

Patience, and I Want It Right Now!

Oh, how many times I have said this
And another has said it back to me
Be patient; all will come about
And in reading and learning from another
Do I know better than he does?

I have finally in earnest tried to get it
But I still have to remind myself all the time
To keep out my human willful pushing
Why, oh why do we allow ourselves
To fall into this trap, so much human will

The key, I think, for me anyway
Is becoming clearer finally
Not to say I have overcome all
But in totally releasing and allowing

The fight is always on, but in knowing
In realizing my tendency to try to push
I then am trying so much harder now
Oh, the many things we need to overcome

But "I want so much right now!"
As I softly smile and reverse this saying
And turn whatever around again
To God's control, not mine

I must continually remind myself
Out of self-arrogance, I go on
It will all come about when He says so
And I, placing myself in His hands
Must humanly and rightfully let go

The Pearl

The pearl is a beautiful thing
So many want to mortally possess it
But let us take a closer look
It has come into being by an irritation

From this process, it becomes something of beauty
Then it needs to be carefully retrieved
What is it worth then, being that mortals put a price tag on it
And then so many cannot mortally possess even one?

Let us now be reminded of something else
Each human being goes through the stages of life
Handling all kinds of irritants a must
And through this process, we each become the pearl

We must allow the healing, the uplifting power
To attain further understanding, expansion of self
Keeping our heart, mind, emotions toward one direction
To the Divine, the source of all, purity of reflection

So if you do not physically have a pearl in your possession
Or a string or two of them or more
It is OK because with the further understanding realized
You have already become a string of pearls with God

PERFECT REFLECTION

If you face a life-threatening situation
Know where your true life abides
Not in this mortal form
But always with God, the Creator
Your soul, where true life is sustained

Declare your love for our Supreme Father
Ask for His help and blessing
Truly believe you are His reflection
Perfect in every way
Ask for and declare His revelations

Our Father, Omnipotent Supreme
Is always here with us because we are one
It is not a dream, an illusion
His love constantly expressed to us
Hold on to His comforting embrace

Truly believe all things can be done
With Him from and with that love
Mortal human form overcome
You are His beautiful reflection
Oh dear child of God

Our human apprehension must be put aside
Knowing that He is our true guide
All things are possible through God
Our Creator, the great I Am

Each one of us a child of God
He keeps close watch over His children
We have not been abandoned
He sometimes has been, though, by us

Know your rightful place with Him
Protected and kept under His loving care
Let not evil influence creep into your thoughts
Leaving your mind full of fear, doubt, or despair

Continually declare through prayer
His reflection, perfect in every way
Know you have His protection and healing power
Lovingly given; lovingly and gratefully receive it

The perfect, beautiful, and whole reflection

Pesky Little Tasks

Why do we fuss so many times
When there is a task we need to do
One that is unpleasant to tackle
But a must to get done
Putting it to the last on our list?

We keep ignoring it until the end
Ever-present in our mind, it is
Until it can no longer wait
It must be completed
"Oh darn," we say

We then tackle the task with fervor
Just to get it done and over with
We roll up our sleeves, as the saying goes
And just plod at it going full bore

As we wade through making progress
On this pesky task of ours
We find that in doing so
The chore seems not so hard after all

Our mind begins to awaken
In the anticipation of seeing the end
It is not really that difficult, we discover
We feel great in the accomplishment

Another triumph over our pesky little task

I am sure many of us are pretty much the same in this. Certainly, I have my share of these little jobs that drive me to distraction mentally, yet they do not go away on their own, so I think about them frequently before I finally address them. This writing came while working in an office for a company, which provided me with numerous petty tasks, but now no longer there, I still find those pesky things remain with me just in living. How human!

Plain Gold Band

I have had the diamonds, the glitter
I have had it all before upon my left hand
No matter what was on my finger, the symbol
The true representation could still be clouded

There has been one in my life, so far
A smaller diamond, he did give me
It was what he mortally could afford at the time
But it was the purist reflection obtainable

Now that he has gone on and left me behind
From mortal existence to the other side
I still cherish the symbol of love
It now sits in among other past glitter

When another true love enters my life
This one will have much to offer
I will ask nothing more than to have
A plain gold band upon my hand

For in living the years I have now
And having other sparkles on my hand
I would rather experience them in daily love
Yes, a plain band of gold will do just fine

The true symbol of simplicity and love
Now fully realized and understood
The plain gold band on my finger one day
The symbol of being fully united

I will already have the true diamond, him

⁂

    While glitter is nice to mortally have, when the symbol comes from the wrong human being, it no longer holds meaning.

Plant a Seed for the World and Watch It Grow

We all have the capability of demonstrating love
No matter where we humanly roam to or from
As we go onward and touch others with softness
Let us plant the seed of love and watch it grow

Each of us doing our part for the whole mankind
Extending love onward to all we encounter and touch
There is no greater power we each can possess
Plant a seed, watch it grow and manifest for all

Each gentle smile, remark, and physical demonstration
Touches and caresses the land, humanity, the soil
We each become an example for others to follow
Plant a seed, watch it grow and become beautiful

Our Heavenly Father planted seedlings, which are each of us
He watches us still as we grow, mature, and blossom
There are many who would perhaps try to inhibit it
The ones who wish to plant the seeds of love will flourish

Plant a seed for the world, as others have done and do now
Each tiny gesture, act of love, and kindness, important
Nourished from our Creator to us who listen and obey
They become another seedling for others to reap and sow

We all have the capability of sowing and then harvesting
We are touched in kind, and others do the same for us
More and more seeds are then planted, then watered
Oh, the reward for mankind is like no other and simply love

After watching and listening to the Yanni DVD *Tribute* and then walking into my beautiful garden, listening to the water flow, I sat quietly and pondered, and then this writing materialized, which encapsulates the flow of many things as well.

Point to Point, the Journey, the Crossing

In this lifetime of mine up to this point
Reflections of the past flood my mind
In looking back, wondering why, oh why
Why did I make this choice and that?

"Where was I at the time?" I ask myself
"What on earth was I thinking?"
Some of my human decisions so wrong
But at the time, I knew no better

I now face the same dilemma, it seems
Wondering about my future decisions
Will I look back and ask myself once again
"Why, oh why did I do that?"

There are so many things I have learned
Some things, though, I still have not
As I ponder, wonder, and reflect on my past
I ask my Creator now for the answers

I have certain destinations in mind for me
Things to do, to be; I wish I knew more
I would love to be able to now state
I know everything and I have it all

But I know that is not the case for me
I must realize that the crossing, my life experiences thus far
Contribute to my continued growth and understanding
Really the most important part to my demonstrations

This poem was inspired by musician David Templeton's CD *The Crossing*, the musician Yanni, and the Greek saying, "I grow older always being taught."

A Prayer: Let Me

Father, this is Your child
Just one of so many created and brought mortally here
Let me be obedient to You
Let me dwell in Your reflection

I will listen to Your quiet voice
Within my mind and deep within my breast
That most precious place, my inner core
Where the radiance of You is softly felt

Let me pause each day, quietly within
Let me open the channel to You each day
Let me dwell with the Most High
Let me become one with You

Let me cast self away
Let me be at peace
Let me love unconditionally, as You do
Oh, Father, let me abide entirely with You

Let me cast adrift all evil influences
Let me reflect Your beautiful presence
Let the radiant glow of sunshine touch my heart
Let the moon cool me down as I become tranquil when needed

Let me express all that You are
Let me stand up with You, the Divine
Let me make You a proud parent
Let me be and do so much in honor of You

As you let me, as I go to You
On my knees with love and gratitude
The humble child that may receive Your loving presence
Let me simply say . . .

I love you, Father, as my connection permits, let me

∞

There are many prayers to our Father. This is one that came to me quietly one evening in reflection to Him. As we all can project and talk easily with Him, let the words flow from each of you, whatever the need is, a declaration for forgiveness, seeking answers, or just positive re-alignment of thought. As we all seek and find the connection each day, His magnification will be made known, and as faith is also declared, the oneness becomes complete. Each human being has the mortal choice whether to stand up or sit down, to continue on with either positive or negative energy flow. There are always times when we each reach a path's intersection for decisions, and although some may be hard, we must continue on with the purging or allow ourselves to be swallowed up and remain in the muck and mire of the negative influences.

My prayer for each reader is that you find your place in the sunshine and glory of His magnification, claim it as yours, and continue on with your individual rightful victories each and every God-given day.

PRICKLY BEAR

I have a neighbor that I call "Prickly Bear" and a nickname only
I am sure he was a nicer man to others at one time, and what a shame
I try to treat him with kindness and a loving attitude, a smile
He, however, does not respond in kind, an attitude always there

I thought it was just something perhaps about me he did not like
And, no it is not; others have told me when I asked them point-blank
He unfortunately is like that to all he encounters, and they stay clear
They try to show kindness, but Prickly Bear remains the same

He walks around with a scowl on his face and a defiant attitude
How sad for him, and I feel that he must be so unhappy inside
I do, at times, think to myself and wonder what happened to him
The outside reflection and attitude of himself from deep within apparent

I guess we all know or have encountered someone like this
They are all over the place, sad but true, and throughout the world
Yes, we try to practice tolerance with our thoughts and attitude
However, it is still up to the prickly bear to change himself

It is just a reminder to me and perhaps to others who are reading this
That our inside attitude, view, and feelings that we have and maintain
No matter the cause or circumstances that brought them to the surface
Impact the perception so much that others have of us

How sad he has allowed his being to become a prickly bear
He is inhibiting his own joy and peace within, as well as for others
I would so love to try to help him be less of what he radiates
And become a softer and gentler loving human being once again

I will try to hold good thoughts for him before our next encounter
I refuse to give up on him and will just pray and know he is God's child
And keep on treating him with love, respect and hold him in prayer
I need to remember this lesson and not become a prickly bear myself

This holds a lesson for us all to learn. I keep this experience close to my being in remembering not to become a prickly bear myself. I am also happy to report that after this writing was released and many other neighbors holding fast with and in loving support, and yes prayers, he has now become, once again, his true self and a loving human being to others. He found his own answers and is now continuing with his life in happiness, joy, resolution, and experiencing many wonderful things, which we are all grateful for. In continuing to lovingly support others, we have to all become mindful of watching for our own inner core, reflections. This is another journey for each.

PRISMS: LIGHT REFRACTED

In my window there hangs something special to me
A beautiful stained glass creation of clear beveled pieces
It is surrounded by a beautiful oak frame
A complete work contained in a large circle

A beautiful design, assembled by another
The love and care taken in the creation shown
Each piece fitting together with intention and purpose
The complete work, the beauty captured within

Different prisms allow light in refraction
Making up the whole and in perfect design
Each selected cut in perfection and joined with others
Then the entire beautiful effect is truly felt

So many different sizes and shapes there are
It is truly a wonderful work of art and creation
When the sunlight pours through it with magnification
What a wonderful result that has been attained

Different colors are refracted and appear in the room
After a while, the clear glass itself takes on color
Absorption of the sun's rays occurring as time goes on
Becoming more intense and adding so much more extension

One has to pause in order to enjoy it, however
In reflection, this object in and of itself
Brings to mind so many other things in retrospect
Realizations for us to gather unto ourselves, within

Each piece, individually making up the end result
So much beauty extended beyond each one
But when they are put together in making up the whole
It reminds me of us in human attainable form

A Promise of Tomorrow from Number Nine

As I often do in my days now by the sea
Looking out over the water in front of me
Listening to beautiful sounds of music
How they touch the emotions
Creating combined power unto me

The mind wanders from past to present
The visual horizon grasping at my being
Then as the mind wanders even more
The visions and promises of tomorrow are presented

As they become clearer, these thoughts embrace
So many possibilities that can and will unfold
It almost takes my breath away, the visions
The warmth felt within from above, overwhelming

I return to the machine that holds the disc
Putting on number nine once more
I do not know the name of the work yet
But the tears are present in my eyes
It does not matter right now to me

As the chords of music swell, then subside
Strength and then softness from its creator felt
Touching my heart and my soul as the work plays
I turn my head once more toward the sea, the horizon

I play it over and over again, this number nine
Being touched by its melody, heart and soul magnified
This needs to be played in Heaven, I say to myself
Thank goodness I can hear it now on earth

As the moon appears and gently caresses the sea
The horizon seen no more and the darkness overcomes
I know within me, however, as I gently smile
It is certainly there, oh, the possibilities of life in store

Was I ready to receive and embrace them anyway?
Or did the music capture my silence within?
Or is it the moonbeams gently caressing the water
The sea to receive them and radiate their beauty?

I do not care in these moments of pure peace
What started the reaction, or was it a combination?
I am so grateful they all came together hand in hand
Number nine, sea, and moonbeams enhancing each other

The treasured moments are captured forever through this writing

This poem was inspired from listening to musician David Templeton's number nine from the CD, *Time Alone*.

There are many beautiful musical works out there for us all to experience these kinds of moments. Find what brings your deep emotions out, and allow them to the surface. You will never know what might transpire in letting go and not only taking your own flight of imagination but also touching base with your inner core to obtain so many things that will surface. The beautiful music that touches you will transform you, bring you peace, and stir the emotions that might be under the surface for either healing or exposing what you may need to finally deal with in your life.

As so many musicians bring us the music from their hearts and souls, let their creativity bring yours about as well. We all have it, so let your God-given direction be allowed to emerge with no limits on what you can do.

Quiet Stillness of the Night

In the quiet stillness of the night
Two lovers embrace and receive
God's blessing of fulfillment
The arms wrapped around one another
The tender moments of love
Each one gently holding on

In the quiet stillness of the night
God gently whispers upon the senses
All is well upon each soul
All is radiant and beautiful
Your expression of Me to behold

I have given to each of you
My own gentle embrace
Upon your hearts
My promise of true love
Passion within
To have and to hold

And when you slumber
In each other's arms
Coming to Me in contentment
I gently breathe into your souls
Oh, sublime peace like no other

The warmth of tenderness
The fulfillment of passion
The truth of Me in each of you
The world to see

And when you gaze
Into each other's eyes
Love, soft love
The expression of Heaven given
The world will take notice and say
"They are one and walk with God's light"

Radiance: Warm Sun, Cool Moon

The rays from the sun filter down
To everything on Earth's floor
Warmth felt, sweet repose
Reflection of Him, open mortal perception

The full moon, cool in feeling
Sending down to earth its own light
We gaze up to enjoy in delight
In the darkness of the night sky

With time, we come to understand
Both have their place to nurture humanity
The grand design by the Creator
The reflective presence from Him
In our seeming darkness

Illumination from both

The Rainbow

The beautiful rainbow
Prisms of light
The magnificent arch
Oh what a delight

It starts and ends where?
We concentrate to discover
Mystifying it is—we watch and ponder
Oh, the colors from the Divine

The story goes, we are told
There is a pot of gold
At the end waiting
For us to find
And then?

What would each of us desire?
In the treasure found
At the end of the prisms of light
Things of the material world
Or Divine magnification?

The imagination takes over
Contemplating such a find
What to do with it all
Blessings hopefully to be derived

What we discover
Comes from searching within
Not from the material pot of gold
At the end of the rainbow

When one is spotted
Know yourself well
Realize our beautiful prisms of light
Are reflected from the Creator

The rainbow is presented
For all of us to share
The rays of the sun
Refracting light through the rain

We are indeed the droplets
Beautiful colors galore
Reflections of Him
Our birthright for evermore
And the true pot of gold

I was living by the ocean, and after a storm, two beautiful rainbows appeared side by side. As I continued to watch them, relishing the intense beautiful colors and trying to imagine where the end of each rainbow might be, their beauty, sense of serenity, and magnification engulfed me, and this creative writing manifested itself.

Reaching for Answers

There are so many things that we hope to understand
On our journey through this human life
So many paths and roads for us all to go on
In trying to obtain our birthright of total beauty within

We think we know the answers given to us at the time
To pause and reflect and hope they are right
The correct path to continue, to be guided on
Our quest to be fulfilled and go onward in His light

We later may discover as time goes onward
That perhaps our answer, our conclusion
Not entirely, after all, is the correct one
Human choices and willful determinations interrupt

We stumble over pebbles on our paths
Trying to decide which answer is the correct one
Will our conclusion to a particular human riddle
Indeed be the correct answer being sought?

Certain things happen that change our minds
We backtrack, waver, again question
The search goes on in trying to at last find
The answers to all of our questions

We at times again ponder our decisions
We then search and wonder about the method we use
In each of us trying to find our true answers
Without becoming even more confused about our questions

We all need to come back to where clarity rests
Which is sometimes subjective at best
We need to clear our minds and know
There is but one source, we must believe
The answers are then firmly given for us

Remain at peace in your heart, the soul at rest
He is ever near, ever-present at our side
The fulfillment of our search readily at hand
He, the only one to be our guide

Be calm and believe God will supply
In humbly asking, you will receive
The answers to your questions
The search itself very necessary
In the process of reaching for answers

Even our correct questions will come to light

    This is an on-going process for each. There was a time in my life that I was not searching for even my questions, let alone the answers. Now that my journey has come to the place that it has, I am continually going through this process as well. It never stops, and never should, as we progress as human beings. Each one of us has to come to a certain place before even the correct questions are allowed discovery.

Realignment, Renewal, the Quieted Mind

When we have fearful thoughts that take over our being
Oh, the heart and soul seem to be in such turmoil
Fear for us or perhaps others, it does not matter
When there are hearts intertwined, the caring still there

There are different kinds of directed love to cause such fear
A parent to a child, the love toward someone special
Love for friends and toward the family of mankind
The negative influences of disruption need to be quieted

No matter the process toward the peaceful result
Humanity has many names, and there are designations
But one thing is certain for all mankind, all of us
The belief in a higher power and the movement growing

Realign the thinking; we must all try to accomplish this
Reverse the negatives, the fearfulness that overwhelms
Renew yourself and pour out the sand of harmful thoughts or actions
Come back to positive belief, energy, and declarations important

Renewal is at hand in doing so for us all and, oh, what peace and joy
It does not matter the cause of the fear or apprehension
The affirmative is the important part to overcome and grasp the faith
To quiet the mind, the being and the heart once more in alignment

Peace within once again attained, and there is nothing else like it
The paths of righteousness, wholeness, our right to possess
The blessing from above peacefully felt once again in doing so
The quieted mind once more is surely felt for us all in gratefulness

We then must express our gratitude for what is received
That is also so important for us to do, to say "Thank you"
Peace will once again be attained and demonstrated, no distinction
Realignment of thinking, renewal, and the positive result for all

The quieted mind possessed through realignment and renewal

A Salute to the Music Vessels of the World

I, for one, salute you all, the music vessels of the world
The music poured out from you to us all
From your beings, your hearts and souls, freely given
We need to all stand up and applaud you, I think

There is such a need and always has been
For mankind to embrace the different rhythms and sounds
Each created work passes on to others beyond even heritage
For each to draw from and affects us, our inner being

Not every work from each and every artist
Will hit the mark, but thank heaven for the choices
But I have learned, myself, over the years
That I need to allow, keep an open mind, then select
I am, after all, the one receiving to be nourished

At times I dismiss one work and on to the next one for what I need
But in going back and re-listening on another day
That dismissed one, by even the same artist, affects me greatly
Each work will either bring me up or gently put me back down

The vibrations and energy coming from each artist, I truly embrace
Resonating within me special things and becoming part of each day
Bringing uplifting emotions or gently bringing quieting presence
The heart and emotion determines what is needed at the time

I wish to express my gratitude to all of them
To all of those that share their treasured creations
And, even though music is subjective, I wish to say
Oh, how many of you have blessed me, and I am so grateful

The choices are ever expanding as others introduce me
To new artists, groups that I have not encountered before
Such a joy they all give to life from their shared releases
There is a bountiful supply that feeds and nourishes me

I hope others will go and find their joy from their choices as well

SIMPLE PLEASURES

Life is so hectic in this day and age; the momentum increases
So many things to do, be, seemingly unrelenting
There seems little time to listen in the stillness
Take in the quiet soft whispers of life, renewal

The simple pleasures, once embraced, now pushed aside
The laugh of a child, innocent, spontaneous, and carefree
Listening to the soft babble of a brook, seek it out
Touching the moss upon the rocks, opposite manifestation

Walking in a forest, beautiful peace, tranquility, the soul touched
Sitting on a beach listening, watching the waves, the froth
Taking the time with loved ones, both young and old
Telling stories of past relished times, holding the hand of a loved one

Listening to music that nourishes the senses and does not destroy
Taking the special times for us to renew in heart and soul
The simple pleasures of life must be visited more often
We need to listen to our hearts and the soft whispers we miss

Enjoy the sunrise, sunset, or a rainbow when presented
Thanking our Creator for the blessed events freely given
Calmness, tranquility, our souls touched once again
Absorbing the soft whispers of life touching mortal senses

All we have to do is allow them manifestation

Soft Memories, Like a Gentle Summer Breeze

You have gone onward now
How I miss you here with me
As I think and remember you with love
Your presence gently with me

When the mortal calendar dates come around
Memories and difficult times, as the heart wrenches
The marking of special events in your life
Oh, how they come flooding into my being

I grieve for you with pain and sorrow now
It has not been that long ago you left
You crossed over to the beyond
To the heavenly restful place

You are with our Father now
In another plane of existence
That understanding itself is healing for me
You are now in His tender and loving presence

I am grateful that I do believe
Some do not have that faith
How empty inside I would be
When the soft memories of you come

As the mortal calendar advances
Each year goes by, and I heal more
The gentle power of the Creator touches me
In soft remembrances of you, I feel the love

I will, in time, be quieter in my heart and soul
Someday I will cry less but gently smile
There may be no raindrops at all from my eyes
When the soft memories of you come to me

I send you my love, as I feel yours
It transcends time and space, never ending
As our Creator is always with us
I feel the soft gentle breeze in my being

You and His healing love

This work was inspired when someone was having a difficult time in dealing with the anniversary of a family member passing on. As I wrote the work in trying to offer loving support, I received additional healing as well. With love, I sent it onward, and love was returned to me, not only from the writing and release but also from the tender appreciation shown by the family to me.

SOMEDAY

How often "someday" enters our mind
Or is propelled verbally to others
In the dreams of wonderful things
That the future may hold in store for each

Oftentimes the years may pass away
The dreams sometimes may fade away as well
In going to our Father, though, through prayer
He can give us the direction needed

Then it becomes the mortal task of each
To not only listen and be guided
But also put forth the mortal effort needed
God can open our doors, but all must walk the walk

With confidence, we can have our dreams
Whatever they may be, to accomplish, possess
In and with faith, hope and knowing it will be
Then patience, understanding of the process needed

In being resolute and with diligence
We cling to our Father to provide
All that we can become and rightly obtain
But always mindful of what the mortal price

Sometimes we want the stars, the sun, and/or the moon
Or even the galaxies far beyond
In perception only, I state this
Then, what price the dream to have?

So in asking for His help
Be mindful of what the dream may cost
In mortal terms, as well as to your heart and soul
Then if the cost be not too much
Make your "someday" a reality when He says

"Now it is time; the doors have been opened, walk"

I have so often said this myself, and thus this writing came, as it was presented to me. Whatever your treasured dreams are, if they remain good and wholesome, in putting forth the mortal effort of alignment with our Creator and in the complete faith that He will indeed guide your paths, He will open the doors. At times, we may even be surprised when they come, how they are presented, and then in clinging to the Divine Presence each and every moment with our own presence, we shall receive almost unbelievable results. As God is the Ultimate Power, we can receive freely in holding onto His hand.

May all your treasured dreams come true, but also remember any mortal price paid from their attainment.

The Space with God for Mankind

The morning breeze has secrets to tell you
Quiet times to be with God, peacefulness
He desires for you to be all you can become
Listen quietly to the still small voice and go forward

The inspiration you will receive from Him
Will enter your mind, your soul, to accomplish
Know that He is always guiding you
Take your rightful place on Earth and in Heaven

Enter God-space, past doors of negative thoughts
Pass through the portals to the Source
Receive from Him your inspiration
Oh, the possibilities are endless for us

Affirm your rightful place with Him to guide
Align yourself with the true essence of Light
Revelations await you with unlimited boundaries
Harmony is felt serenely with God, the Source

Receive in full measure what you desire to accomplish
For the good of mankind, for you to reveal
Others will be blessed by what you do
While you in kind will be fulfilled beyond measure

Speak No More Of . . .

You have physically departed from me now
Your visit of today now over
The words you spoke to me
Come back to haunt me, however
Thus, I must write my thoughts down

The emptiness you express repeatedly to me in your way
Even anger, frustration, loneliness, and more
The talk of the lost, abandoned, and dead love of another
Now you just want the act of physical release
And you say that with little emotion attached

As we talk and thinking I love you
I cannot tell you that now, and it cuts to my core
I do not have that right, you see, and just listen as you share
Your hurt is my hurt, and the pain I feel is great
I wait for a true love myself, you see, and all that it can bring

I had one, but he departed to our Father a few years ago
How I miss the soft moments shared
The tender embraces are greatly missed
I too, you see, have much love still to give
I feel so lost at times; oh, Father, please help

I wait with emptiness, longing, and desire
Just as you are going through now for another
I have been praying while thinking I loved you
Oh please, God, send me another true love
So that I may share and have the void filled

Dara Marie

Mortal time just keeps marching onward
I am busy with life but still feeling empty inside
You have appeared but still belong to another
The things you say, share with me as just a friend
Cuts my heart in half at times, and you do not even know

For you see, I think I love you and beyond just passion
Remain though I must, silently making my testimony to God
How I do, would, could love you even more
I would tenderly treasure the times we have together, as I do now
Such as they are, as just friends

In good times and when dark clouds might appear
Hand in hand with love and faith in each other
With God, we could overcome anything
But I must, for now, remain silent except to God
I know He hears me, as I put my faith back where it belongs

I cannot show you this writing
As you lament for another now in your life
She helped you emerge long ago to an expanded awareness
But things did not last for the two of you
And now all I want to say is . . .

Please speak no more of . . .

    As it turned out, this person was not the one for me. I lamented, as do many when encountering someone like this whom they think they love, but as I look back now, I realize God certainly knows better. This person still remains in turmoil, but I have long since let the situation heal itself . . . for me. God does know better, but it is hard at the time to relinquish ourselves as we should when the human emotions are involved.

SPINNERS

As we ventured forth on our chartered boat
Upon the crystal blue waters near Maui
All of a sudden the spinner dolphins came
Pod after pod, they gathered together

How playful and free they were and are
Such magnificent creatures of the Creator
Their freedom was so joyous to view and absorb
As they gathered together and joined us humans

They listened to the chants of mortal calling
We celebrated them and voiced it over the waters
Sending them our love and paying tribute
Oh, wondrous mammal children

As the humans cried out from their pleasure attained
Relishing in the beautiful performances before us
Leaping out of the water, spinning, and turning
As if to say, "I bet you wish you could do this, human"

They darted about, this way and that
Through the crystal-clear blue water off Maui
Teasing us with their hide-and-seek routine
And then breaking through, once again, the surface

Oh, the freedom and playfulness they display
Makes the heart and soul of a human being soar
Oh, thank You, Creator, once again
For giving us such joy in watching and loving the spinners

DARA MARIE

Spiritual Black Sand

Oh, how incredible the place
Approaching the sacred beach
Gingerly making my way down
To the sacred black beach on Maui

The large waves crashing full force
Then water, froth with foam, upon the sand
Gently caressing the shore, movement
As if to gently kiss and deposit back more

I slip my shoes off, my bare feet now in the sand
I cannot wait to get them in the warm water
To feel the soft touch of the combination
The powerful water and the sacred black sand

How beautiful and sacred this place is
The energy felt from all of the elements
Oh, how Creator blessed this place
Still relished by all who visit

Many are in the water as I approach
Some swimming carefully because of the currents
Others standing waist high in the blue water
And joyfully giggling as the wave energy thrusts them backward

Others just bury their feet in the sacred black sand
The black pebbles shimmering as the sun kisses them
The whole cove so very beautiful, oh sacred area
Thank you, Creator, for yet another special spiritual place

As I stand there quietly within myself
Just drinking it all in and absorbing others
I close my eyes and try to imagine
The sacred, loving, and pure past ceremonies on this place

Moments and minutes turn into hours
I drink it all in, watching others partake as well
Listening, feeling, sensing so very much
Purification of all human beings while here, evident

When I finally leave, I say farewell
I will return here to partake even more
Pictures were taken of the area
But I have them firmly placed in my memory

The peaceful expressions and gentleness upon each face
When human beings finally makes their departure
Surely demonstrates the blessings received
They carry with them the treasured experience

Being on the spiritual black sands of Maui

Surrender

In gratefulness and soft surrender
I stand at a new door
Letting go and releasing
My heart and soul

In direction, sweet meditation
Surrender
Full heart, full soul
Expressions of you
Flowing outwardly through me

Contemplation, resurrection
Passion ignited
My cup now running over
A larger one needed
To be filled
Refractions of light

As the sunrise develops
Beautiful colors presented
Radiating outwardly from the Source
All to see, all to absorb
To grasp, to understand

The yearning to learn more
Passion pursued
Absorption, manifestation
Feelings united—life
Boundless enthusiasm
Possibilities unlimited
Mind opened

The special place
To receive
Joy expressed
In love's tenderness
Gratefulness, humbleness
The sunrise awakening the sleep

New thoughts, ideas presented
The clarity unfolded
Small steps taken
The faith renewed
Letting go, continuing on
Oh what joy, anticipation

As I found myself in soft surrender one evening, these thoughts quickly passed through my own being, and I hurriedly wrote them down. At times, this is all it takes to capture what we feel deep within our own core for surrender and liberation.

Swept Away

When things in our lives take over
Turmoil seems to encroach into our very core
The test of our faith that we have
Must be firmly declared, absolute

Whatever it may be that is presented
We feel swept out to sea at times
The unending expanse, where are the answers?
On and on, we feel cast aside, adrift, alone

There are the uncharted waters so many times
All of us are faced with them now and then
The feeling of being so totally lost
We need a chart in which to navigate

We are like something just bobbing up and down
In the vast expanse of a sea, lost, without direction
We cannot see a shore, the land, solid ground
But we all know mentally it is there waiting

Instead of flailing about, the mind racing
We need to somehow calm ourselves down
Declare our oneness with our Creator
He is the Chart, the Navigator
He knows and gives good directions

The shore, the destination for us to reach
Is indeed there, even though we cannot see it
More headway is achieved in absolute faith
Our needs will be provided for in all things

The sea of life, the expanse of it all
Sometimes makes us believe and feel
We may never again obtain landfall
But in persistence, calmness, faith, we can

One stroke at a time, resolute and with intention
Using our true Navigator and maintaining our faith
That He does provide the right directions for us
We are taken care of, and we reach the land

No fear; cast it aside once and for all
Your Navigator has proven He can overcome
In releasing and letting God guide and listening
The journey so much easier to our correct destinations

    This poem was inspired from the composer/musician Yanni's "Swept Away."

SYMBOL OF GENTLENESS, PEACE, AND BEAUTY: RENEWAL OF MY HEART AND SOUL

A morning of feeling heartache and pain from outside forces
Swelling over me like a huge wave, fully engulfing me
I was treading water emotionally, my heart wrenching so
Then going to the window and looking out, gasped with surprise
There you were, peacefully resting upon the grass, form hardly seen

I felt the darkness of my heart decrease a little, as the sun rose higher in
       the sky
As the symbol you represent, your presence came into my heart
There you were, one lone doe quietly visiting and resting
As if to say, "I am here to touch you in a most special way
You have sent love my way before; now my turn to give it back"

As the dawning of a new day progressed, more light entering mortal realm
Slowly escalating, revealing, and I just watched you for a time
I thanked you for coming to my land, for appearing this morning
For you have no fear, concern here, as I have welcomed you before with love
I also thanked you as more beauty and peace came unto my soul

As I continued to just stand and watch you from the window
Then more little ones joined you; from where they came, I do not know
You just watched over them; on guard you were, but in peaceful presence
As the rest of your family went about grazing upon the land
Then you all progressed on your way, as the day itself advanced

As the darkness contained deeply within me was being released
Renewal of positive emotions now surfacing once again
Your symbol of gentleness, peace, beauty, grace, and oh-so many things
Flooded over me, within my heart and soul, renewal once again
Yes, renewal for yet another mortal day now upon my presence

I thank you and, of course, the Creator, my Father
When I needed something to softly embrace, as the pain was great
You were provided for me to touch your presence, as if a reminder
Life does have softness, gentleness, beauty, and peace
Now I can pick myself up once again for healing ways

How I needed to see you this morning, and it was as if you knew, somehow
As the past days have been weary with heartache for others' pain
Now someone close to me just did not understand something I needed
           from her
She did not consider how I might have felt or even inquire
I looked at you, smiled, and also thanked Him for bringing you to me

Yes, she, too, has been caught up in something as well, and I understand
But, I was reaching out to her and got no support for my heart, feelings
Yes, my fragile being is showing now, crawling back into my shell to heal
There was no reaching out to me that might have helped in my hour of need
Or having the thought that I might have needed something other than
what she did

I now release to my Creator tears of gratefulness once again
Yes, it will take a little time for me to fully come back
But with the soft gentle touch in my heart and soul once again
I will regain what was lost, become stronger, and continue on
Renewal once again, and started with the touch of a single doe

The Symbol of the White Dove

The wings of the white dove take flight
Circling overhead to God's delight
Bringing such beauty and grace
For all to see and witness

Up, up, and away it flies
Circling and demonstrating peace
The white dove in beautiful motion
I glance upward, a smile on my face
Oh, God's wonders performed for us to witness

To remind each who behold
The white dove of purity and love
How tender and warm each heart becomes
As God smiles and says, "Well done, My dove"

Peace, love, joy to all who embrace
The dove from God so firmly placed
In human existence for us to be reminded
Once again of His love for His children

An example it is of how we should be
Beauty, gentleness, purity, grace, and above all
Love's reflection in serene bliss of flight
Toward the horizon it gracefully glides
Onward to God and to be held with love

Tapestry of Life

Colors, textures, and weaves in mortal life
All incorporate the tapestry I show and wear
Each human being has his or her very own
Advancement, understanding, life absorption

The colors reflect who and what we are
How we embrace the triumphs or pitfalls
Positive or negative thoughts, reactions, words, or deeds
Create the changing tapestry we represent

Some colors darker than others, events of life
They could represent depth or darkness of being
Others are brilliant, radiant, and glowing
From triumph over mortal strife, attainment

As each tapestry may be different somewhat and/or unique
The threads of the tapestry may, with time, change as well
Coarse or smooth, dull or shimmering, and/or intense
Our individual tapestry can change but never unravel

As life has presented many things to me thus far
Challenges, relished memories of beauty, even despair
To the top of mountains but also into the valleys, even the desert
Each thread and color of my tapestry has had meaning

Sometimes, I cannot decide about my threads or colors
I now have lived mortally long enough, the tapestry somewhat lengthy
I know there are many different threads and colors in my own tapestry
I do hope it is beautiful enough when I finally go to my Father

And as He looks upon the presentation, I hear, "Progress attained"

Tea Kettle, Oh, Tea Kettle

I put you on the stove this morning
Full of pure water you were, as I needed
For my breakfast instant oatmeal, oh well
I am now so in need and very hungry, oh my

Then off I did go while you were sitting there
The heat turned on, water to release steam
"Hurry up," I then declared and departed
Now, as you whistled at me so, I said
"Shut up—I am busy now; you are bothering me"

Oh, the sounds of your shrill voice, piercing the air
Relentless you were, as if to say, "I am ready
You filled me up with water; now come and get me
That was your intent, as you placed me upon the burner"

"Oh, oh, I am coming now," I yelled at you, "cease the racket"
Greatly irritated by it all, as I had become involved with something
As I took you off the burner and turned it off, one twist
I was still greatly irritated but wanted and needed your end result

As I was then full within, your hot water helped provide me nourishment
"Oh my, tum tum feels so much better," I said to you and myself
"OK, I am sorry I fussed so, and you did what I asked of you
The end result was asked for and needed; thank you"

As I sat there, talking to a material tea kettle, another "oh, oh"
I suddenly got the thought, "Oh my, what am I doing?"
It was as if you were indeed a living thing, a being
Oh, I have too much alone time on my hands, I was thinking

"I'm sorry," I said automatically to you
Even though you are just a material metal container
I somehow felt badly in my words directed to you
As you just sat there now quiet, I was appreciative that I had you

I will treat you more respectfully in the future
After all, I did ask you to perform a task that needed to be done
As your bottom was heated up; hope you don't mind
I need to let you cool off, clean you up for next time

When I ask you again to do something for me
And, when you call me with your shrill blasts
I will be most appreciative that I have you at all
And, the water in which to fill you up, some have not

Now, as I do, my mind wanders and wonders at the same time
Gee almighty, if we do this to God/Divine
When asking Him to release and perform what we ask, need
Am I going to, with human will, not like the answers I might indeed receive
Tell Him to cease, as well, in mortal irritation?

I simply now will say to you, "I am coming"
To you my material tea kettle now sitting there quietly
And in performing what I ask you to do for me
Why on earth would I give you my attitude, after all?

As I just smile to myself, the mind has taken me far
Just from this silly conversation to you from me
As I step away and go on with other things to do
Did I hear you say to me, "You are welcome, and you have a better attitude"

At times, the simplest things can trigger something for us when
we allow the imagination to flow. In thought and reflection, we can
contemplate many things, even with and from a material object as this.
I no longer am irritated when I am summoned from the whistle and just
gently smile. That, in and of itself, is a relief to me, as I go and retrieve
what I had wished to be produced in the first place.

Tears of Mankind

We are all in one place
Upon this planet of ours
Gazing up at the stars
Reaching our souls to God

It matters not where each soul resides
What part we inhabit
We are all one under Him
Reaching our souls to Heaven

We all need to pause for a moment
To reflect and meditate in our way
To be oh-so grateful
For yet another wonderful day

Mankind needs to be reminded
Every once in awhile
That our existence here
Is by His will, not ours

Every species here on Earth
Part of the whole plan
Each one having its place
In the great scheme of things

Mankind is the ultimate
Free will has been given to us
To go in one direction or another
Oh, let us all go on the right path

We can choose this way or that
Human reasoning at time incorrect
When the wrong path taken
We then cry out for help

Wouldn't it be so much easier
For each to say first
"Dear Creator of us all
I will listen to your voice
Help all people to heal and be healed"?

If each one of us did that
How much more joyous our lives would be
There would be no more need
For tears from pain and anguish
Tears of gratitude, joy, and peace
Would replace these

In embracing the concept, "we are all one" on this earth of ours, and touching base through my heart and soul for other human beings, this creative work took life. As our world expands but shrinks at the same time with technological advances, we truly see what others go through as well, as human beings, what is happening to Mother Earth, and how it makes no difference what part of the globe we inhabit. We are all affected, inter-connected, but all having, as well, free will.

I will always remain optimistic that mankind will eventually come to terms and choose the direction needed for peace, prosperity for all. As our Creator, the Light, is greater than the darkness, more human beings need to come forth and declare their oneness with that Source beyond religions and maintain the tolerance needed for each other. Thus the trials of and for mankind continue.

Tears of Pain, Tears of Joy

Look upward toward the sky
Cry out if you must, even on your knees
Toward Heaven's gate opened
Teardrops flowing freely, mortal release

There are many drops shed
Over a life from strife, from joy
The heart and soul of each mortal
Can experience more unity with God

As needed emotions are released
He knows the pain in each drop
He knows the joy released as well
Come and visit more often, if you will

No self-pity or shame in the concept
As each drop cascades down upon the cheek
He has given this release to us
So that we can even demonstrate what's inside

As a gentle breeze blows upon the land
Or hurricane gale in forceful demonstration
Each kind of tear has a special purpose
Oh, the cascading water at times

How sweet each tear is, though
Whether from grief, sadness, or joy
If each one could not be released
How the soul of each would seem as dead

So release those tears, man or woman
It is good to do so, now and then
He already knows the kind they are
Because our Creator has given us the capacity

Do so in sweet release, and be not concerned

 This writing came to mind after someone dear in my life, in talking of her father and being somewhat reluctant about shedding tears so liberally, was feeling so badly in doing so. I hugged her, tried to comfort her, and this writing was produced when I returned home as I thought about tears and what they can do, stand for, and the purpose for the release for us all, man or woman.

Tender Love

Oh, tender love, how I wait
For you to appear before me
A gentle touch and warm embrace
There could be oh-so much love

A soft, gentle smile on your face
The eyes soft and with warmth
Expressing all that you are
All that there can be shown and done

Your kiss so sweet, signaling the beginning
To feel you and finally just be
In sweet tenderness, oh, the joy
For at last, I now have my true love

Where have you been?
So long I have waited for thee
To fold gently into your arms
Surrender by and from your love

The longing, the anticipation over
Now you are finally with me
The wait is over now
We are indeed as one

We must have not been ready before
God knew the best plan after all
Now that it has been unfolded
We both thank Him; He knew best

Each one complete at last
The other fulfilling the love needed
We then now go onward
With Him, our lives are blessed

To be witnesses of His love
Patient we both were
What beauty and joy now to experience
And radiate the love we now have

For all to see and know
Each one blessing the other
Doing, sharing, and just being
Oh, so much in pure love

This creative work was inspired from all the loving people I have encountered over the years that had patiently waited, longed for that very
special someone to enrich them, bless them, and enhance them with and in
full radiance. This is also, hopefully, inspiring for those still waiting.

There Is Another Day

When life pushes at us in so many things and ways
We have so much we want to do and accomplish
The unending bombardments from the outside world
We never feel we are caught up or making any headway

We all have our secret desires and wishes, future achievements
Things we would like to pursue and accomplish
In this time of the world wanting instant gratification
We all need to learn to calm down a little more perhaps
There is and will be another day when something can be done

The real test for our goals, our dreams to become manifested
We need to never let our passion die or wane within our being
If these things we want to accomplish for just us are to materialize
If they are truly important enough for us to hold close to our hearts
Their time will come through our own patience and persistence

We all need to keep our focus on the things we truly desire
Always tackling what we deem the highest priority for the day
Then the rest will fall into their rightful place, headway made
The appropriate method, resolve, and timing, so important for us

We always seem, however, to run out of human time, we say
Or are our dreams, our goals really on top of our list?
We at times need to rethink and delve deep inside us
To initiate the first important steps

Then with resolve within us, we can all push ahead
Toward our dreams, our individual goals to attain
One day then flows into the next one toward results
Before we know, the success is ours in the endeavor

When the goal is personally reached, whatever it may be
We must all be grateful and not let ourselves forget the passion felt
From when we first started the process for attainment
Now the realization of success is finally at hand

There is another day to behold and achieve even more
One step at a time in reaching toward our dreams, our goals
Then that dream, that goal is behind us, and then there is another day
Other demonstrations to unfold and be realized—sweet success attained

Things Foretold, Then Mortal Reality

Going to a higher presence beyond mortal being
Having another foretell of things to come, perhaps
Events, people to play a large part in our lives
We believe all as told to us, or do we, should we?

Then when we feel all will come true as conveyed to us
Certain other events out of our control may change
Or is it our perceptions, our imaginations that take over
When particulars, told to us, do not come to fruition as expected?

Where do we draw the line from blindly believing things predicted
      by another
Or relying on our true connection to God, and letting Him unfold
      the future?
Something we are told may even then throw us into total disbelief
Because we were so sure something was going to transpire for us
Perhaps literally hoping something happening in just a certain given way

We are taken aback a little or perhaps thrown into a tailspin
Is our destiny truly what we have been told or believe?
The forecast of so many things seemed so wonderful
And now, since something did not work out, the doubts presented

We may struggle in believing what the ultimate unselfish goal is or should be
We constantly may go back and forth mortally with emotion
Have we been just told another grand story by another human being
Or what we are to accomplish here in the mortal plane, reality?

So many wonderful and glorious things would transpire
For not only us but also for so many others from our deeds
I guess it comes down to one basic principle
Having faith in what was foretold by God directly to us only

And then allowing Him to guide, bringing about His reality

The Ticking Clock

The clock ticks in its own rhythm
Evenly paced, one tick after another
Human time being erased
Our lives here on Earth departing

We all are fully engrossed
In daily tasks that need to be done
Our minds controlled in the moment
Oh, but what of our destinies?

The outward world consumes us
So many things to tend to
We must all pause and reflect
Be mindful of the ticking clock

If we were not so immersed
In our daily grinding routines
What would we do with our time?
What would be important to us?

We each must make our choices
Live to the fullest extent of us
Or let the clock just keep on ticking
Life gone by in retrospect
Will there be regrets at the end?

While I was trying to start a new life of being single again after my husband passed away, I was sitting quietly in the living room listening to the antique clock that he loved so much. I was in contemplation of my own new direction, and this writing came into creation. In looking back to where I had been, I realized there was now a new beginning, many new opportunities of life being presented if I chose to step forward. Yes, I was no longer in the same place, but in looking back, I did find my own regrets of lost time for many things and no longer wanted to be feeling that.

DARA MARIE

Time Alone with Him

Time alone can be so reflective
If the heart and mind are peaceful
One can quietly ask to be guided
His direction is always and constantly provided

Ask and you will receive from Him, the great I Am
The messages gently expressed to thee
Take heed when direction is given
You will just know your questions are answered

Then we humbly have to recognize
To be able to go on in faith and trust
To allow ourselves the freedom
To react upon the answers given

To have resolute faith in Him
Knowing full well we will be taken care of
Our journey continues onward
To bless others as we are in turn blessed

If everyone did this here on Earth
To their Creator, Father of us all
Think how wonderful and beautiful
Our human world could become

Each human being reflecting
The love, the caring, and the great I Am
Each soul sharing with one another
The beautiful fulfillment of true man

This poem was inspired from musician David Templeton's *Time Alone*.

Tiny Seashells Cast upon the Rocks

As I sit here on a rocky beach in Greece
Quietly communing with God by Messinian Bay
Grateful for so many things He gives to all
I looked down beside me and found you there

Nestled in-between the stones, you were
Almost hidden from view but yet there
Tiny little seashells of all kinds
Brought from the sea and gently deposited

I picked you up, so tiny and fragile, you are
Putting you gently into the palm of my hand
I kept looking at you in wonderment, head tilted to the side
How on earth did you survive the journey to here unbroken?

The sea gently deposited you among the rocks
You could have been destroyed or at least harmed
But you were completely all right, fragile, little shells
Oh, how tiny and sweet you really are

Thus my thoughts wandered to us as human beings
When so many outside elements can dash us to the rocks
The grace and love of our Father, however
Can and does protect, shelter, and guide us to safety

Gently and lovingly, we are protected as well
From the rocky shores of life we may encounter
That would try to crush or destroy us, His gentle ways known
Even the Divine Father protects fragile little seashells from harm

Do you not think He does the same for His children?

DARA MARIE

Treasured Friends

As we go through the mortal journey
Many human beings we encounter
Those that impact us now and then
Those that have wandered onward

There are a few who move us more
Our hearts and souls are tenderly touched
One to another, we are all blessed
We are nourished, flourish, and are fulfilled

It seems to be so rare now
In this day and age of human time
To have those that truly are considered friends
Friendship that lasts a lifetime

Some say they are our friends
But in the test of life encountered
Circumstances and situations presented
Few make the final extended grade

Treasure the ones we have
They are unique and so rare
They are always there for us
No matter what in life is encountered

True friends are always there for one another
Through thick and thin, as the saying goes
They are always there for us
No matter how graveled the roads

They may disagree with our decisions
They help us whenever they can
By deed, word or through prayer
The helping hand is always extended

There are many human treasures
That one would like to obtain
But a treasure beyond compare
The treasure called a true, lasting friend

A Tribute to Greece in Honor of Yanni

The mountains standing strong
Upward to the sky they climb
Ever onward to the Divine realms above it seems
Reaching towards God's sun

The sunlight piercing in-between the clouds
The kiss of light awakening the outlines
The moon still seen as well in the sky
Both lights in unison creating breathtaking wonderment

The low clouds like white feathers
Gently caressing the ground with a kiss
The warmth from Mother Earth
Creating the fog, moisture escaping, combining

The beauty of the land I see
So green and full of life and promise
The rocky areas highlighted from sun and moon
Bringing forth the comparison of earth and senses

Greece is just awakening from slumber
A new day for all to unfold
The smells and sounds of life
A new day of blessings to partake

What a glorious land this is
The Greek gods presided over long ago
The warmth of humanity
So much agape . . . love

The beauty of the land
Even inland from the sea
So much history of mankind
Here in this place called Greece

Looking down from high above
The beautiful green valleys below
The small villages tucked here and there
It makes one ponder all of the history here

So many generations
Standing firm, proud, protecting the land
Not allowing anyone to continually conquer them
Oh, what a people, oh, what a land

Gently descending from the mountains
Going toward the sea once again
The two blending and becoming entrancing
Water so blue and pure, oh Greece, wondrous land

Such a powerful presence there is here
So much life and ages gone by
The world so much more enlightened
From the strong, resolute, but gentle people found

So proud of their birth, their heritage
They are Greek and love their land
The feeling arises, though, once again
The world encroaching on their old ways, identity

They want and need to have the good things
Others in the world have attained
To get ahead and provide more for their loved ones
So much is started, but money so elusive

These proud souls of Greece stand tall
Some may leave the land for a while
Better opportunities elsewhere may call
But their hearts always remain here

For this land nourishes their soul
Always calling and bringing them back home
The mountains strong, giving them unusual strength
The surrounding sea providing freedom, their souls released

It will be sad to leave this land
This placed called Greece holds something special
One can feel so at home here
Even though so many things are different

A gentler existence, the pace of life in harmony
The rhythms of the day with more simplicity
The world can go on for a while
The love of Greece fulfills the needs of their soul

I hope to return to this wondrous land
There is always so much to see and absorb
From a land so full of strength
The beauty overwhelming, the gentleness, serenity, love . . .

Agape

    In my two visits to Greece, the people and the land touched my heart and soul. While taking a bus ride back to Athens from Kalamata on my first visit, this writing was given its birth, and I include it in the book as a tribute to the musician Yanni and the people of Greece.

    When one particular area of the world affects us so much, a writer must release the emotions and the truth of what they have discovered. Other creative human beings do the same through their pictures, paintings, music as Yanni has done in tribute to his birth country, or other artistic endeavors with and through their passionate inspirational outlet.

Find the places where there will be such an impact on your heart and soul, cherish the memories, and find your artistic arena in which to draw them forth so the treasured moments will not escape and become lost. God has provided so many places here on Mother Earth for us to embrace, explore, and receive astounding feelings that one may not even be aware of them, let alone the people, cultures, and the wonderful diversity of the human beings inhabiting the land.

The True Gift Given and Received

Oh joyous time of year this is
Mortal celebration of great love
The material things given and received
Just a small part of it all, it would seem

The greatest gift I can give
And the one most cherished from you
Is not wrapped up with pretty paper
It does not have a bow or ribbon upon it

Give me no material thing to receive
Presents can come and go over time
Give me your love, as I give mine to you
That is what means the most and lasts

Give me the love from your eyes
A sweet touch, gentle hug, and embrace
Love far more treasured than even gold
These expressions last the test of time in my heart and soul

To experience laughter with one another
To know you love and care as I do, even through tears
The most important thing, no mortal measure
Give me your heart and love eternally, as I give to you

I give you back the greatest gift I can
In letting you know in different ways
How much I truly love you, family or friend
No pretty box, paper, ribbon, or bow
Can contain the pure gift between us

Beyond this time of year, day by day
Let us continue to touch one another
Even in and through simple things
Love always being exchanged, not like some presents

There is no greater gift that can be given or received
It has no method of measuring and is worth so very much
For it is of such immeasurable treasure
As the true gift given and received

The greatest thing, the never-ending gift of love

As the holiday approached in December, my daughter said to me, "I don't know what to get you." After I said to her, "I want for nothing because I have your love," this writing came into being. This could apply to any marked personal event as well. Yes, it is nice to receive a material gift, but when love is not present, obtaining a material possession leaves us empty deep inside. Without love behind it, the contents of a beautifully adorned box represent and hold only emptiness.

This writing was given to my family that Christmas morn, and as tears flowed, there was a most treasured group hug, which all remember, as true love was expressed and received.

TRUST IN THIS DAY AND AGE

How many times in this day and age
There are so many things and others
Whom we may encounter in our daily lives
The trust issue and concern always present

All of us have had our trust issues and realized disappointments
But, thank heaven, others have fulfilled their commitment
It becomes difficult at times to really know
Who and what can be trusted as presented to us

Are they truly what they say they are?
Is it only to propel themselves through mist and clouds?
We, however, can always know and declare
When they do enter our lives, we have God's protection

They will try to deceive and guile, say anything
Trying to make themselves something they are not
But holding on to the declarations of protection
They will show themselves as they truly are with time

In one form or another, we will surely know
From others we trust where deceivers have proven who they are
Or perhaps from that inner voice of warning, red light flashing
That little siren going off within each of us

It is sad that deceit seems to be escalating
I can remember stories, for example, from the past
Of the times people just shook hands with a smile
When an understanding struck, whether personal or business

Now there are so many more emerging things
Our civilization becoming so much more advanced
Legal issues, products, people more complicated
Oh, wouldn't the simpler life be grand now? Looking back

Distrust seems to be perpetuating with such force in every way
Coming from every direction, it would seem at times
But in being able to trust in the Ultimate One
That will and does provide for our protection when we listen

DARA MARIE

Two Lovers in Heaven

Softly spoken words in the night
Two lovers holding onto one another
The darkness of the room comforting
Quiet contentment, time so cherished

Both quietly thinking to themselves
How wonderful and peaceful
This must be how Heaven feels
Or is it just because of us?

A sweet kiss upon one another
Each moment so sublime
Wrapped up tightly in a sea of love
Waves gently caressing the shore

"Oh, how wonderful you are," each one says
"My life so fulfilled now
My life so blessed and radiant
How grateful I am for you"

As time drifts away into the night
Two lovers still intertwined
The kiss of God upon their souls
The feeling of Heaven on Earth
True love given and received

The Ultimate in Giving, Unconditional Love

There are many things we can give others
Whether they are family or friends of ours
Material items to be possessed and be treasured
But the ultimate giving to one another
Unconditional love, is always cherished above the rest

In giving to one another through this kind of love
In and through whatever means is needed at the time
To uplift someone else, whether directly called kin
We are all the Creator's children in like kind—no separation

A smile, a gentle touch, understanding to one another
To hold firmly to positive beliefs and spread wisdom onward
To support one another, each human on earth so important
To embrace differences of cultures, how we each live and believe
Unconditional love that our Creator holds for us and demonstrates

We may even disagree with human determinations made by others
We would do something entirely different ourselves, we think
Each human being, however, has to listen peacefully and in faith
To his or her own heart, drawing upon the known Source

It is hard to let others go onward at times
Their conclusions, understanding may be far from ours
We have to be patient and truly consider their point of view
In having our own conclusions, viewpoints of life
Can we say we are always in the right, or ours the only way?

As long as there is no harm to others in the process
Being extended from beliefs different from our own
Love has no boundaries, but being in mortal state
We try to place them into our reality; we are the right ones, we say
Each one of us may think we are, but perhaps we are not

It is so humanly difficult while each one on the journey
Through this life, trying to understand all that is presented
For humanity, mankind as we know it now here on earth
On the brink of seeming disaster, all of us being affected

We need to understand the larger picture for us all
The ultimate price that could and would have to be paid
In our human insights, in and through human ignorance
Unconditional love, as our Creator gives us all in the great giving
The one constant, ever-present reality, Divine demonstrations

    This poem was inspired from musician David Templeton's "The Giving" in tribute to his father, and in honor of Sotiri and Felitsa, who passed unconditional love onward to the world as does their son Yanni through his own work for mankind.

The Uncluttered Path

In going after our dreams, our worthy ambitions
We cannot expect, nor should we
To have God drop everything into our laps
With no human effort produced from us

We should pray for our protection
Our direction and guidance; He will supply
Listen to and with the heart within
Listen to and with the calm mind

Recognize and allow your path provided
If truly the right one for you to go on
It will come lovingly bearing fulfillment
Given from Him, demonstrated by you

As long as we cling to God, the all-knowing
And continue to honor Him with humble gratitude
Our destination good, pure for us and everyone
He will grant our wishes, dreams, and ambitions

Have faith when answers are given
To you lovingly from Him
Through your mind, your heart and being
You will know where to start
You will know what to do
Your path cleared of obstructions

Be mindful, though, of how and why
Your destination is to be accomplished
Take precious care of what was given
Be thankful and give Him your love
Your path to Him will also be uncluttered

Uncomplicated Love

Why do so many
Think love so complex?
In being a couple
Both hearts should be blessed

At times each one ignores
The true beauty within
Or does not fully comprehend
One's love's inner soul

Each heart yearns for happiness
Contentment, and joy
Why is loving someone
Seemingly so difficult?

Treat your loved one
As you would like to be treated
Love the other as yourself
Each of you can still remain unique

Each heart should remain
In beauty of one's own
Each one giving of oneself
As God does from His throne

Each life combined to make one
Through love eternally given
To be cherished by the other
Pure love transferred to one another

If the waters of your life are stirred
The waves crashing onto the shore
Do not forget how and why
You fell in love with each other
Cling tightly together and know
You are one in love

In your love's reflected beauty
The turbulent waters of life will subside
They will come ashore once more
In gentleness and perfect rhythm

How simple it would then be
If each person would embrace
Love's purity, goodness, and grace
As God bestows to us all
In tenderness and abundance
It need not be complex after all

United with Pure and Lasting Love

We all dream of finding the perfect one for us
We try various methods to look for our special someone
That one person that will gently touch our being
Magnify our heart, our very core, and the soul of us

We, at times, look too hard, always searching
Perhaps rationalizing some things with our mind
That the person we may have just finally met
Might, indeed, be the very one we search for

We may even talk ourselves into some feelings
That, perhaps, do not really exist for another
In our human desires, needs, and longings
To find that perfect someone just for us

We need to be fulfilled and be whole ourselves
To understand our being, our deep place within
To be as solid as we can, first and foremost
Then our soul mate can be gently placed before us

We also must have faith in the Creator
To give ourselves to Him and be gently directed
To know that our someone, that special person
Will lovingly be presented to us by Him in time

Then we must look beyond the outside image
Deeply touch and comprehend the beautiful inside
To go on in unison, growth, and natural blending
And, in the reflection of each other, love united

For each one to blossom and become a beautiful half
The blending in and through love the main ingredient
To establish what is called lasting unity from true love
Our soul mate, how wonderful for both, when found

It can last a lifetime in keeping God first for both

WAITING

As you go through your work shift
Waiting for the call to help
The bell rings out to summon you
The signal for you to respond

To be of service for others
To lay your human life down
To rescue, protect humanity
It matters not if you know them

With love and dedication, you serve
You put yourselves in harm's way
You work through your assigned shift
Waiting for the bell to signal you

No matter what may occur
You diligently work to save
It matters not if only property
But the lives you save more important

In doing your job, in completing your tasks
Each member of the team so important
You also lay down your life for each other
For your fellow brothers and sisters

There may or may not be fear
The challenges presented unknown
You put on your gear and just go
When the call, the bell rings out

Humanity calls you heroes now
Especially after 9-11 transpired
I believe you are so much more
Even though a fireman now gone said
"We just do our job"

Waiting is at times boring perhaps
There is, however, always something to do
To keep yourselves sharpened in your skills
In order to perform the tasks required

To protect one another from harm
As well as rescue property and human life
There is no greater deed asked of us all
Than to lay our lives down for another

So in closing and completing this tribute
To all the firefighters of the world
I again say, "Well done and thank you"
God/Creator is looking down and also saying

"A job well done, My children," as you wait for the signal

  This writing came about after 9-11 in knowing what my late husband had accomplished during his own career, but it is a tribute to all the firefighters around the world. Let us not forget what is done by them, as well as all the others who protect us in their own dedication of service.

Warmth or Cold

Sun streaming through the windows
Yet it is snowing outside; how strange
How marvelous a sensation this is
The true beauty and wonder of it all

The wish that it would continue on
This wonderful feeling I have now
When two separate events as this
Occur at the same time

I cannot make up my mind, however
Which one I would rather have
Glorious sunshine to fill the heart
The warmth of the rays to receive

Or the gentle beautiful flakes falling
In such wisps of ballet in the air
I stand transfixed and just observe
The beautiful peacefulness of all obtained

The emotions of what is happening
Thinking and feeling how special it is
Not wanting the warmth of the sun
To melt the large, beautiful, white flakes

Time will tell which one will win
The warmth of the sun or the white lace
I will hold this in memory by writing
It is one of those very special moments

The Water of Life

Each Divine droplet so tender and dear
Mortal human being dipping into the Divine well
Life eternal to be withdrawn and claimed for all
God's promise truthfully unfolded and magnified
Each glass for the soul, filled to the brim

Each time we go to Him once again
A larger glass needed for our heart, our soul
Further understanding of life, truth, and love
For our true being to be replenished from Him
Oh my Lord, oh my God, in gratitude we are

As we travel on, our mortal journey unfolded
We will indeed understand His messages
We must be still, and then we must listen
The quiet voice gently given
In love and grace we meditate until
Our glass is overflowing once again

We are then offered an even larger glass
To be filled yet again with all God provides
Again ever constant and filling us within
The Divine water will indeed help us overcome all

The water of Life from the eternal Divine well
Freely given to each human being
All we have to do is make the choice
Partake, drink, and allow the nourishment

Oh, love's tenderness
Oh, how sweet the embrace
Everlasting, from Heaven's gate

He pours forth the water of life
Through thoughts and feelings received
The peaceful heart, oh, how sublime
Gentle beams of light divine

Through His mercy and truth
Life, love, and the light of understanding
In soft communion with God, we are
No separation, no part of us untouched
We are indeed one with Him and bonded for eternity

Our Creator looks down from above
His tender messages spoken so gently
His guidance freely given to all who ask
With open hearts, with bared souls
We go to Him and are blessed

We do not know for certain
The future remaining a mystery
But hand in hand, we go with Him
Our glass will always be lovingly filled

Honor Him with your heart
Honor Him with your soul

As He gives us the sunrise
Understanding of Him awakened
Nourishment to gently embrace
Beautiful days of serenity and peace
Freely provided from above

We are His children and reflections of Him
Never-ending fulfillment to be attained
Mortal man entering His kingdom
I give you my love, oh Father of us all
In sweet embrace, love is indeed all

When at our sunset of mortal life
Heaven's gates are opened
His loving arms outstretched
Enfolding us with sweet tenderness
Smiling and saying, "Here I am
For I am the great I Am"

We, as droplets, then become streams
The streams then become rivers
Emptying into the Divine place
To be renewed and then turn around
To replenish someone else again

In love and truth, we know His word given
Proven with demonstrations throughout time
Oh, the Divine, given of God
The pure water of eternal Life

Waves in Faith

The longing of a lifetime
Reflections of the past
Comes in waves over me
Like the ocean upon the shore

Reflections of time gone by
The waves of renewal
Generously given, gratefully received
The blessing of His love, ever-present

The understanding of a life no more
Steps on the journey, the basis of renewal
Preparation for the life ahead
Oh, how I feel the light from Him

The journey ahead for me not clear
To be unfolded as a sunrise or sunset
The beautiful and radiant colors
Oh, love from Him expressed

In complete and quiet faith
My heart and mind be still
I wait patiently for His direction
Oh, the life of renewal to unfold ahead

I will not question His direction
In my eagerness, I anticipate
To grow and be like a beautiful flower
My soul to partake the love given

WE ARE ALL THE SAME

No matter where we are
No matter where we may roam
We are all the same
In unity and love
Under the same throne

We all must go to Him
Our Creator, whatever He is named
In gratefulness and quiet reverence
To the great I Am

We should realize we are all the same
All His children, His reflection
Protected and directed, we ask
Uplifting our hand to His
For His guidance and love

He is always near, ever-present
He is never absent, but we are at times
We must reach our hearts to Him
Searching for His loving ways

Mankind of each region
The blue marble is our home
We call Him different names
All the paths lead to the same throne

We are all the same
Each child of Him unique
We all desire the same things
From the Father of us all

We all cry, grieve
Have joy and love
All the same human qualities
He has given to us all

It matters not the tone of our skin
Our speech different from others
Our customs, our dwellings
Each region unique on our earthly home

We are all the same
Seeking the same love and comfort
From our Creator above
What the difference of man?

We are all the same
In our Creator's eyes
We are all loved equally
No matter what the outside appearance

Each nationality unique in its ways
He does not distinguish
He loves us all equally
We are indeed all the same

When Mortally I Go Onward

When my Father calls me home
Until my soul is, perhaps, to return again
Spread some of my ashes, and fling them into the sea
Over the water that feeds my heart and soul

By this time, you have already said goodbye
To the mortal shell; my true essence has gone on
You will feel me still because my love is with you
I am always near, now just in spirit form

What I was able to do this time around
The touches of and from love toward others shown
Let that be my true legacy and carry it on
Love reflected in love, the true reflection

Because of my love for you, always present even now
Spread the good tidings onward, and feel me always with you
As your heart and soul are touched in remembering
I gently send you mine back from above

I am now spirit, one totally with the Father
When it is time for you to come toward the throne
My loving presence will be waiting for you
Until then, the unconditional love remains as always

I will send sunshine to your heart
I will also send you moonbeams during dark hours
Hold all tightly to your heart and soul
And feel my loving gentle presence with you

Even if tears flow down your cheeks
I am in those drops as well; we are indeed connected
A gentle embrace as I wrap my loving presence around you
Uplift thyself, and go onward to your waiting destiny

You have much to give the world and mankind, the love
From your gentle inner presence reflect Him
The Divine in all things as you have possession of it
I have no greater gift for you than my love

My presence is always with you, my dear ones

While it is always difficult to write something like this, I do feel it is important to leave our loved ones something from the heart and soul of each one of us when we do depart to our Heavenly Father. My family will see this when the book is published, but I will also leave it to them on beautiful paper and gently seal it with a kiss. I did want to include this writing for the message and purpose it contains.

Write your own beautiful farewell before it is too mortally late and seal yours as well with the love you have for your family. As the years pass, they will have it from you, along with the memories, and it will comfort them for their remaining time of mortality. Love transcends time and space, so let your message to them be made known, and they in turn may leave their own message when they depart, and so it goes on, as love does.

White Diamonds

As I look over the vast water in front of me
The beauty of the area glistening in the sun
The water reflecting the rays like diamonds
The seagulls floating and gliding on the airwaves

The boats leaving safe harbor and venturing forth
Their destinations known only to their captains
I quietly stand, watching them depart to open sea
Gently they make headway, parting the white diamonds

I feel so lonely watching them go on their way
How I wish I could be with them and be on the sea
Gliding over the beautiful crystal, shimmering, blue water
Over the white diamonds parted by the wake

The beauty of the area and one of God's wondrous creations
Is here for all to absorb and relish in peaceful bliss within
To find the peace that perhaps has eluded them
The soft breeze from a perfect day gently caressing

How I wish I could partake and be on one of them
The wind in my face, disturbing my hair, I do not care
To be with others as they experience the same
The glistening white diamonds parted, complete freedom

I need to remember, though, that even if I feel alone
A feeling of almost being forsaken by others
God is with me in my heart and soul
In my whole being and while watching white diamonds

I will have my turn one day; this I know
I feel the peace as I imagine being out on the calm sea
To look down and cut through the beautiful clear water
Pausing and closing my eyes in thanking God for such beauty

As the different vessels come and go in front of me
I need to remember God is always present
I will know that, yes, one day when it is time
I, too, will have my turn upon the blue water

I often think how it must have been
Before mankind encroached upon this land
So peaceful it must have been
The white diamonds undisturbed by man

The seagulls would glide as they do now
In peace, grace, and freedom
The only sound would be them calling and gentle waves lapping
God would whisper, "All is joyous, peaceful upon My land"

Mankind, please take note as you embark upon the white diamonds
Take care and be watchful not to harm in any way
The sea, land, or the animals you encounter
To not disturb or destroy what God has so freely given

A Work in Progress

How many things life has presented
Some ups, some downs, turning around
Challenges, feelings of defeat
Also ecstasy when seeing defeat turned into victory

I sometimes fall backwards, I feel
At least it seems so many times
But, as advancement of thinking through things
I come back into alignment with my Supreme Father

We must not give up or give in
Sometimes we may want to retreat
As the outside world's waves of upheaval
Come crashing down upon our shore, our inner core

If I feel the arrows sting my heart and soul
And question my own ability to arrive at the answers
I look to my inner self with quieted thoughts
And with humble gratitude realize I am a work in progress

So when again my steps do halt in forward motion
I have the choice of which direction to go
I can remain in doom and gloom
Or keep ever watchful of my work in progress

Nothing worthwhile is attained easily
Against any negative forces I will not relent
Each person can select the direction for his or her future
And I have chosen to advance and not look back

I realize I am a child and remain humble
Even where and when great mortal strides are made
I bow before my Supreme Father
That my work in progress be sustained

Forgive me for my transgressions
Forgive me for my backward steps
Forgive me for my seeming failures
Forgive me for so many things

As a child, I do wish to reflect
All that You are, all that You wish
So please be patient with Your child
Your work in progress from Your love
Thanks You for Yours, Almighty Father

You Are My Horizon

As I stand here at ocean's edge
Looking transfixed to the endless horizon
You hold the promise of things to come
In the distance you call to me; I hear you

The tremendous waves coming in with mighty force
Slight wind thrusts the spray upon my face
I close my eyes to embrace it all in the moment
Letting go of time and space; they are forgotten

The feeling of renewed endless possibilities await
It penetrates my entire being with so much power
Bringing a sense of pure joy to my heart and soul
I open my mortal eyes once again

You are the beautiful reflection of love
And I am yours with heart and soul
You touch me like no other presence
Hand in hand, we are one in unity

The feelings run deep within me
You make me feel beautiful like no other
You are the promise given
Love, life, and truth to behold through you

There are no boundaries between us
I have your love, and you have mine
Mortal life sometimes seems as a dream
But you are my horizon for endless possibilities to unfold

You are my horizon, unlimited, all encompassing, and all love.

∞

The subject can be both our Father and our most special someone that
is anticipated coming into our lives when there is no one already present.

Your Search from the Depths of the Inner Core

I hear your soft cries, tears gently cascading down your cheeks
Sitting quietly by yourself, wondering about so many things
Even though we are apart, the connection in place
You are delving inside your core asking to receive and heal

So many things have been building up over time
You have dismissed and pushed them from your heart
Pushed them aside using a broom, the complex mind
Now the intense emotion over time will not let them go

You have been able to achieve so much thus far
Now you are being forced and placed in an area of pause
Reflections and pictures from the past are flooding in
There are things for you that can no longer be swept away

You close your eyes, the gentle tears rolling down
You feel someone, the warmth though upon them
You are asking yourself what is this feeling
A parent perhaps is communicating with you now

You know where your true strength resides
A strong being you possess and a gentle presence
But at times we all need to come to a place within
He guides and heals in His way and brings us to our knees

You will be renewed with time, and that is His promise
Listen to the angels as they speak to you as well
You are now finding your way with these things
Deep inside you the emotions of missed blessings

Time will heal, but you now need to pause and listen
As a message was given to you a while ago, now
Find it once again, and you may discover within your heart
The hidden answers that He passed on to you

Dara Marie

POEMS BY KIMBERLY LORRAINE

These works were composed by my beloved daughter, Kimberly Lorraine, between the approximate ages of nine and fifteen. I hope you enjoy them. Such is the purity of expression from one so young, and this mother is very proud indeed. All of her poems I have typed as Kimberly wrote them.

ALL OF THESE THINGS

And when you need me
I'll be by your side
Draw you close to me
With nothing to hide

And when I whisper
Gently in your ear
I will take away
All of your fear

And when you stare
With love in your eyes
I'll look back
True love recognized

And when I love you
Each and every day
I'll tell you now
I'm here to stay

And when you slip
I'll catch your fall
I'll be here always
Whenever you call

And when I speak softly
Only to you
Believe these words
I do love you

And when you are breaking
And need a friend
Stay close to me
I'll help you mend

DARA MARIE

And when I dream now and then
I'll have your love all over again
And when you know all of these things
Then you'll discover what true love brings

Enough Time

If there was time enough to tell you
How life would have been
I wish I could have met you
Or just have been your friend

It passes by so fast
Not leaving time enough to tell
Whether we're going to Heaven
Or whether we're going to hell

If there was time enough to tell you
How things have worked out
Would I have to whisper?
Or, would I have to shout?

It passes us by so fast
With nothing to hold onto
The time has come to say goodbye
Without forgetting who had loved you

If there was time enough to tell you
That everything would be fine
You know I would have told you
But, there wasn't enough time

Feeling Free

I have this place, my hideaway
Where there is quiet in my own way
Where I can be my own self
Where I can live without a care

Where I can be lazy or sad
That's when I write with pen and pad
I have this place, it belongs to me
That's when I write just feeling free

I'll Love Her Forever

I love her smile
And the way she talks
Her funny laugh
And the way she walks

I love her jokes
The good and the bad
Her silly little grin
When she's been had

I love her eyes
So blue and clear
She's cheery and bright
And so sincere

I love her wiggle
When she's pounding rocks
She's a dummy
Doesn't know when to stop

I love her for her
Because she's unique
She's not quite normal
But she's not a freak

I love her voice
She sings so well
The louder it gets
It rings like a bell

I love the time
We spend together
I hope she knows
I'll love her forever

I love her not because she's my mother
But, because she's herself
And there ain't no other
And every moment with her is special

Mother's Day for Mom

All of us are special
In each and every way
But it takes a mom like you
To make boo-boos go away

I could say I love you
But that wouldn't be enough
'Cause you are always there
When the going gets real rough

You are always patient
When we're at our wits end
But most of all you are
A very special friend

If I had to choose
Between you and another
I would always choose you
Because you're the #1 mother

Dara Marie

Mother's Day for My Grand-Mother "Moffa"

I don't want to share
The special thing I've got
A grandma nice as you
Whom I love bunches a lot

You have a certain flare
In everything you do
And that's why you're special
Just because you're you

I don't want to trade
Baseball cards or gum
Because you are priceless
And that's why it's fun

You are the best there is
A model to look after
You fill my heart with love
Kindness and laughter

NEWLY DISCOVERED POEMS

The following four poems by Kimberly—"Homeward Bound," "She," and two untitled ones—I found in my mother's things and, until then, had no idea Kimberly had written them at the age of thirteen.

Homeward Bound

I'm homeward bound
Running away to somebody's town
I'm homeward bound
Searching for love, hoping to be found
Making money by writing my songs
Hoping for a dream just to sing along
I want to go home, don't want to stay
Don't wanna be reminded of yesterday
Homeward bound
Running away to find some way to say
I love you

SHE

She's pretty, she's bright
She's young, she's light
She's nice, she's sweet
She's kind, she's neat
She's love, she's literate
She's great, she's considerate
She cooks, she keeps
She yearns, she weeps
She's joy, she's faithful
She's prayer, she's grateful
She's all these things rolled into one
Guess who she is . . . why
She's my mom

Untitled 1

Together we have a lifetime to share
To say how much we really care
Sharing our dreams, promises, and all of our hopes
It'll be a long hard climb up a very steep slope
To face and avenge new horizons
To challenge and conquer without any doubt

Our love is as strong (soft) as a white feather
Precious and floating
We'll stay together
Not my words, but by a bond
As fresh and clear as a crystal pond
A lifetime ahead, a challenge to make
A handful of courage; give and take

　　　DARA MARIE

Untitled 2

Looks like I'm alone again
Talking and crying for a long lost friend
Nothing to fear, nothing to hide
You took all but my love and pride
You left me standing cold, and alone
Didn't tell me what I did
Didn't call me on the phone
I'm gonna make it
I'm gonna be alright
You know I can take it
So give up the fight
I'm gonna make it
I'm gonna be alright
And though you won't admit it
You are finally seeing the light

POEM BY LUCILLE ELIZABETH

My beloved mother, Lucille Elizabeth, passed away in 1984. She wrote this on the Fourth of July, 1983, and sadly, it is the only work I could find after her passing that she had done. I include it here in tribute to her.

EVENTS AT THE SEED BELL

Two purple finches came to my table
Cautious and careful, the seed bell to wobble
But chipmunk had come just a moment before
To stuff in his jowls sunflower seeds, and much more

Then towhee came with his catcall cry
Descending with such fury
He frightened that little chippy guy
Who jumped down in a hurry

But alas that towhee was not to be
The one to celebrate victory
For along came ravenous, clumsy crow
Aggressive, forbidding, a formidable foe

He bullied his way with a caw, caw, caw
But a most brilliant color that you ever saw
Came frightening like a lightning flash
That hummer buzzing made ole crow dash

The tiny hummer never had a need
For anything from that bell of seed
But he seemed to feel it wasn't fair
For so many to quarrel and not share

From there he flitted away to sip
The syrup I'd made for him, then with a dip
He tried the nectar in a bloom
As he flipped his tail, went away with a zoom

Aren't we all sometimes just like that
Even deterred by a tiny flying bug
That buzzes and whistles in our ear
We slap at it with a fancied fear

324   DARA MARIE

Sometimes we angrily give up a goal
And flee, then later regard the toll
That we have paid and henceforth regret
To have given up, the challenge not met

We pray, "Free us from our human strife"
And that is good throughout one's life
But why not know that things can be
Go faithfully on and see
What He has planned for us in His great love

A joyful happening from above
For there is nothing but one's golden calf
To hamper His purpose in our behalf

THOUGHTS FROM THE AUTHOR

The world is more than we can fully grasp. We often question why so many things happen to us and to our fellow human beings upon this blue marble called Mother Earth. With so much hatred going on, battles between the light and the dark intruding forces, emotions of upheaval surrounding us and tugging us here and there, we can find peace within ourselves and know our Father loves us. We can claim the Divine energy flow as the supreme force.

Every human being has been given the ability of free will. All have the choice of how we relate to one another and how we treat our Mother Earth. We can choose to live in harmony, show respect, possess tolerance, act with grace and dignity, perceive with gratefulness the beauty and bounty of all things, and maintain loving prayers for ourselves, our loved ones, and all humanity. The collective consciousness means we are all one, we are all connected, we are all here on the same planet, and we all have the responsibility for each other.

As our Creator, the Divine Energy Source, is always ready for us to come and experience the revelations we may need, I pray with all my heart and soul that you claim that truth for victory over any situation. As our Father is always ready to give everything beautiful to His children, let us also manifest Him and reflect His beautiful essence to the best of our ability. Each time a kind gesture is done, each time we just smile to another, or each time we pray, it is well with that Divine energy, and our action is given back to us. The law of attraction works.

So many things are manifesting with ever greater speed upon humanity. Let us all come together each day in the collective Divine consciousness and continue to radiate love, understanding, and patience for each other while also standing up to the dark side with thoughts and actions of reversing what is transpiring. Each person does make a difference as we collectively extend our positive thoughts and prayers continually outwardly to the cosmos. The positive energy alone makes a difference, and we need to do it each day as we embrace the Light and discard the seemingly dark forces that would try to take over our hearts and souls. We must all fight diligently against these forces, as we many times allow that energy credibility and existence, and declare our Father is the supreme one-and-only force. If we state that God is all good, all love, all truth, and all life, then He is in fact all. There is no room for anything else—He represents all. Unity of people, no matter what our spiritual beliefs or practices may be, still makes the difference as we declare we are one, and love is our common bond. We all wish to get to the same Divine source.

As we go to our Father with faith, humility, and gratitude with our requests, we are provided our rightful Divine manifestations. There are times, though, that we may think something should transpire in a specific way or indeed at all, but in continuing to maintain that faith, being obedient to His direction, we can also discover after the fact that having our way was not the correct one.

I also believe it is necessary to pour out the sand—negatives of any kind—from our vessel so that we can have the wonderful Divine pure water of life flow into us. When the negatives are purged from our being, then we allow the resulting space for the purity of the Divine elements. As we reach toward that Divine energy and become one with it, we are renewed. The sand, any element that is not of our Father, is eliminated from our thoughts, our attitudes, what we do, and for our ongoing growth and attainment. We then have more space in which to achieve and make our triumphant demonstrations.

There is never a time limit on this, as our Source always welcomes each heart and soul and surrounds us with abiding love. Reversing negative thoughts at the moment they try to intrude upon us is important, as we can get a negative force stuck into our minds. The negative emotions that then arise can greatly impact our lives if we allow them dominion over us. We need to get to the point of instantly recognizing them and automatically reversing the negativity.

We are all truly a work in progress.

ABOUT THE AUTHOR

Dara Marie was born in Illinois, and at the age of one, her parents moved to Seattle, Washington. She presently resides in the Olympic Mountain Range on one and a half acres just outside Sequim, Washington. She has one daughter who lives north of Seattle, as well as two granddaughters.

At the age of three, Dara showed an interest in the violin, so her mother provided private lessons at the age of five, and she played in her various school orchestras until going to college. Although she was offered the opportunity to compete in dance-style roller skating, Dara decided after watching various coaching sessions, seeing what the skaters dealt with in the sessions, and realizing the harshness contained in them that it would impact the true beauty and release of her skating experiences, and so she declined. She never regretted that decision. Dara also studied ballet from the age of six and became involved in dance to the age of eleven when the violin took precedence. All her experiences in these artistic avenues proved invaluable in her appreciation of beautiful music, artistic expression, and the sense of the Divine elements being magnified in her heart and soul.

Having had various careers, Dara's accounting ability finally won over. In her last position, she wore several hats for many years—financial assistant controller, as well as payroll, human resources, and accounting manager—for a corporation in Bellevue, Washington. Being very grateful that she could leave and retire early from the company, she did when her writing ability started to transpire.

After her husband, John, passed away in 2004, Dara came to a crossroad in searching for and determining what her future life should become. She grappled with life-assessing questions. What had her life to that point really meant? Who actually was Dara Marie now? What did the future hold? What direction should she take? And most important, what was the true sense of her inner being that had been hidden away so long?

With a spiritual background instilled from her mother, Dara went quietly to God one early morning, opened herself up to the Divine Source energy, and totally released heart and soul. That Source called to her as if to say, "I have the answers to your questions, your direction. I do have all that you need. Come to me, the great I Am, and receive." Her intense, spiritual, quiet session with God that early morning lasted for over two hours with her total release of self. Dara went to a whole other level beyond mortality. She also has written of that experience in "The Release of Me," which is incorporated in this book.

Dara has been given many revelations after that, even a prophetic ability demonstrated through reality, and still continues on her journey of spiritual exploration. She still considers herself a work in progress and feels we all are. As a reminder of this for herself, she wrote, "What should we do with the knowledge attained? We have to absorb it, then use that knowledge, and through our lives absorb all the more for our advancement."

After being directed by the Divine Source in whom and what she should read toward her future enlightenment, she began her studies of the more expanded spiritual aspects. In quiet surrender, she has also obeyed many Divine directives, and all have provided the exact answers and the exact timing to receive the manifestations that were needed. Some even surprised her and took her life into a whole new unforeseen direction.

A few months after the death of her husband and while still pursuing her spiritual re-awakening for advancement, the first writing came to Dara in July of 2005. It was directed to a specific human being whom she had never met. She was told to show it to three specific people, which she did. Each one said exactly the same words to her, which in and of themselves had some shock value. They all said, "You have received this from a higher source. You don't write like this, so mail it, and then let it go." This Dara did. Then more writings started. Although Dara had no prior experience with this kind of writing and even had trouble composing a business letter, she continued to release on to paper, and thus finally this book has now become a reality.

A whole new direction for her life has been made. From her experience in drawing from the Source, Dara is always amazed at what can happen, but understands the why and how of it all. She knows it is never too late to start something new and gain a whole new direction in life by letting go and letting God direct her path. Now she relishes in her new unfolding destiny. By allowing and being in service to and for others, a wonderful glorious new path and life has opened up. She remains truly grateful for all that has been and will be bestowed upon her in the future.